1 14.50 A2
W9-AQW-597
CANADA
M4Y 2R5
WITHDRAWN

RISKING CHRIST FOR CHRIST'S SAKE

REGIS COLLEGE LIBRARY
100 Wellesley Street West
Toronto, Ontario
Canada M5S 2Z5
WITHDRAWN

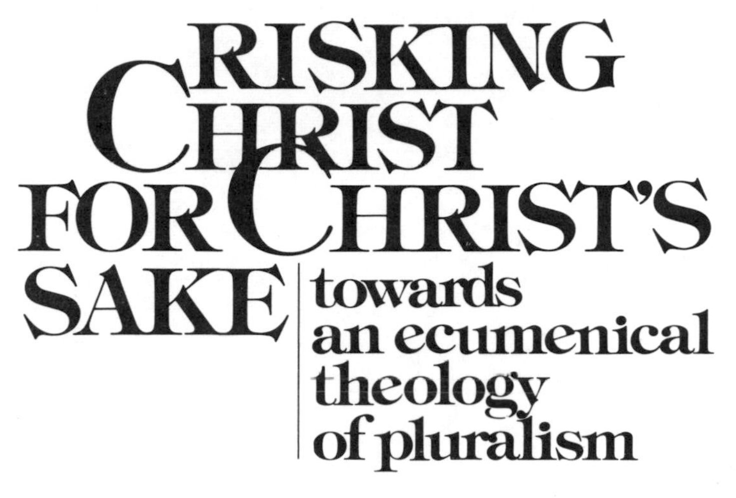

RISKING CHRIST FOR CHRIST'S SAKE

towards an ecumenical theology of pluralism

REGIS COLLEGE LIBRARY
100 Wellesley Street West
Toronto, Ontario
Canada M5S 2Z5
WITHDRAWN

BR
127
T518
1987

M. M. THOMAS

Regis College Library
15 ST. MARY STREET
TORONTO, ONTARIO, CANADA
M4Y 2R5
WITHDRAWN

WCC Publications, Geneva

95534

Cover design: Rob Lucas

ISBN 2-8254-0882-4

© 1987 WCC Publications, World Council of Churches,
150 route de Ferney, 1211 Geneva 20, Switzerland

Printed in Switzerland

Contents

Preface

The churches today face no greater challenge than the one they encounter in the situation of religious, cultural and ideological pluralism. Within their search for human community and in their effort to redefine the meaning of Christ, the church and the Christian mission, this challenge is most real.

This booklet is basically an enquiry into the theology of pluralism. It has two loci — the ecumenical movement and India.

Raymond Panikkar and Paul Devanandan represent two significant streams of Indian theology in dialogue both with India's pluralistic consciousness and their own Catholic and Protestant traditions. Within that setting they have made their unique contributions in exploring the meaning of Christ and the form of the church of Christ.

In the World Council of Churches Devanandan initiated discussion on interfaith dialogue on the basis of his experiments in dialogue under the auspices of the Christian Institute for the Study of Religion and Society. As his associate it was my privilege to work with him and share his theology of dialogue.

This book is a personal recollection of that collaboration. It is also a spin-off from a more comprehensive course of studies on the gospel in a pluralistic world which I have given, first at the Andover Newton School of Theology in 1981 and later at the Princeton Theological Seminary in 1982, 1984 and 1986.

My thanks are due to friends in the publications department of the World Council of Churches for undertaking the publication of the book, especially to the publications editor who took a personal interest in preparing the manuscript for publication. If obscurities still remain, it only shows that there are limits to what a busy editor can do when the author is impossible.

January 1987 M.M. Thomas

1. The Challenge of Pluralism

The pluralistic situation

There has always been a plurality of religions and cultures in the world. In the past religions and cultures have lived largely in isolation from one another. What is new today is that they have moved from their separate, isolated existence to what may be called a dialogical existence.

Many forces in the modern world have contributed to this situation. The most obvious is the technological revolution which has converted the world into "a global village". The development of communications technology has made the peoples of the world next-door neighbours.

The period of Western expansion into Asia and Africa was also the period of Christian missionary movement. Missions introduced the Christian religion into societies which until then had experienced little religious diversity, thus giving rise to religious pluralism. As the West introduced European culture through education, old cultural and social values underwent substantial changes. Western culture was in various stages of secularization, and accompanying it were rationalistic and atheistic ideologies. This meant that the Western impact brought to the non-Western world many ideologies, some of them opposed to all religions. Thus the pluralism of secular ideologies, which had become a feature of the Western world, was also exported to non-Western societies.

In the nineteenth century non-Christian religions were, in general, passive. The anti-colonial movements in Asia and Africa resulted also in the awakening of non-Christian religions and world-views. The discovery of the riches of Eastern religions and their scriptures by scholars from the West has contributed to this awakening. Later, Hindu, Buddhist and Islamic missions emerged in the West, attracting converts from Christianity and bringing about a new religious pluralism in the traditionally Christian West. Christian churches in African and Asian countries and converts to Eastern religions in Western societies have both been seeking to root themselves in their respective religious cultures and thus become indigenous.

The migration of ethnic and religious groups across national and continental boundaries enhanced the pluralistic character of all societies so that pluralism today is not merely a global phenomenon; it has also become local and national.

Large percentages of the population of European cities like Birmingham and Frankfurt are made up of non-Western peoples who are adherents of non-Christian religions. Early immigrants to North America were drawn from the churches of Europe; and it was this plurality of denominations among the Christian immigrants that led to the establishment of the United States of America as a secular state. But the USA since then has attracted ethnic groups from all parts of the globe, so that American society today is religiously and culturally more pluralistic than ever before.

The emergence of nation states and the notion of religious liberty in Europe can be traced to the long drawn-out Catholic-Protestant hostilities which could not be resolved through armed struggles. Citizens could now choose any religion or reject all religions. In our day, religious liberty has been recognized as a fundamental right of the human person. It has found expression in the UN Declaration of Human Rights. The Roman Catholic Church officially accepted it at the Second Vatican Council, thus explicitly declaring that the traditional institutional tie-up of religion, society and state in medieval Christendom is untenable at the present time. All traditional societies are moving towards the recognition of ideological and religious diversity. This raises the question as to how, in such a situation, religions and ideologies may move from mere co-existence to cooperation in building communities, and what common basis such cooperation should have.

This is the issue of dialogical existence in the modern world. In India, for example, in the face of the religious and communal rivalries, the only viable option is that of the secular nation state; but the question of building a national community is only raised by it, not solved. That is in fact the problem of social existence everywhere in the context of pluralism. It is so not only for nations but also for local societies and even for the global community. The global problem is that of building a world community of peace and justice in an ideologically pluralistic world.

In short, the forces of modernity have destroyed the isolation in which religions and cultures have been living traditionally. They are compelling us to live together in the world as one community. It is the awareness of this compulsion that raises religious, cultural and ideological pluralism as a problem in the global village.

Of course, even in such a situation it is possible for people to build spiritual ghettos in which they may live in isolation from one another. Or they can follow the path of aggression with a view to dominating others. Both these are destructive and possibly self-defeating options. The only creative way out for humankind in the modern context of pluralism, it seems, is for each religion, culture and ideology to recognize that people are in a situation of dialogical existence, and to explore the possibility of cooperation and pro-existence, without in the process losing its own ultimate spiritual basis.

The confessional standpoint

Our task in this book is to understand and interpret this pluralistic situation, especially the religious and ideological pluralism we encounter globally and locally, from the standpoint of our ultimate commitment to Jesus Christ as the revelation of God.

Any ultimate commitment is of course accompanied by many penultimate commitments, and finds expression in them. This is as true for Christians as for others. The search for human community is one such legitimate, penultimate expression of the ultimate commitment.

There are other such legitimate standpoints which provide perspectives to understand our pluralistic situation. For example, universities in many parts of the world have been surveying and interpreting religions, cultures and ideologies, as part of their commitment to the rational, scientific exploration of all phenomena. Thus today we have approaches to the study of religion and religions under various rubrics — science of religion, comparative religion, phenomenology of religions, sociology of religion, psychology of religious experiences, philosophy of religion, history of religion, etc. They are all efforts to examine the religiosity of humankind, and to make sense of it and its various expressions.

We have had many developments within these scientific disciplines through the years. When a mere "objective" observation of religions was found inadequate to do justice to a realm where subjectivity is of the very essence, these studies have sought to consider what a religious tradition means to those who live by faith-commitment to the truth-claims it makes. Wilfred Cantwell Smith has gone to the extent of saying that the science of religion should do away with the category of "religions" and study the "faiths" of persons.[1] This, however, has not been universally accepted. But the point — that even a rationally objective study of religions should concern itself with the subjectivity of persons and peoples within the religious traditions — has been recognized.

Nevertheless, the rational understanding of religion and religious pluralism can never satisfy a religiously committed person whose faith assumes that rationality is conditioned and becomes idolatrous when pursued as if it were unconditioned. For such persons, whether adherents of religions or secular ideologies, ultimacy lies only in the interpretation of pluralism from the standpoint of their own faith-commitments, that is to say, only in "theological" interpretation, *theos* here being understood as the basic ultimate reality.

A believing Christian will recognize the legitimacy and the relative validity of rational explorations and interpretations only on the basis of his or her faith-commitment. In fact there are many Christian scholars who move to and fro between the rational and theological interpretations. It is difficult for the same person to keep the ultimate-penultimate boundary line intact, and often there is a certain tension between the theological and the rational. While the theological understanding of religious pluralism requires rational data for critical reflection, rationalism, so far as it is itself a faith-commitment, can easily undermine its own exploration. And conversely, theological commitment may not be held in sufficient suspension to enable a rationally objective selection and evaluation of the data. Therefore, serious conflict results when the scientist or the philosopher consciously presents his or her method and conclusion as ultimate, or when the theologian rejects any legitimacy to a relatively autonomous science or philosophy. Eric Sharpe in his book *Comparative Religion*[2] gives ample illustrations of this problem.

A professor in the Department of the Philosophy of Religion in an American theological seminary told me once that when Karl Barth visited the seminary, he questioned the legitimacy of philosophy of religion as a discipline in a Christian seminary. Barth was aware of the danger of compromising the *sui generis* character of the Christian revelation when interpreted as an expression of the natural religiosity of humankind. Many, however, would contend that it is a necessary discipline to avoid this very danger; it will show the penultimate character of philosophical enquiry and the distortion of truth when that character is ignored. That is, it will show it within that discipline itself.

The debate between John Hick and Lesslie Newbigin on the approach to inter-religious relations is interesting in this connection. In his Younghusband lecture on "Christian Theology and Inter-religious Dialogue"[3] Hick distinguishes between what he calls a "purely confessional dialogue in which each partner witnesses to his own faith convinced that his has absolute truth" and a "truth-seeking dialogue in which each is conscious that the Transcendent Being is infinitely greater than his own limited vision of it and in which they accordingly seek to share their visions". He is convinced that Christianity must move emphatically "from the confessional to the truth-seeking stance in dialogue". In his *God and the Universe of Faiths*[4] he calls this move a "Copernican revolution" in theology involving "a shift from the dogma that Christianity is at the centre to the realization that it is God who is at the centre, and that all the religions of mankind including our own serve and revolve round Him". That is to say, openness to God in inter-religious relations requires that Christians do not start with a Christian faith-commitment to the centrality of God's revelation in Christ.

Newbigin questions this approach. He says that in the realm of religion there can be no neutral standing ground. Any position one takes is a position of ultimate commitment. Newbigin points to "the logical fallacy" involved in the position:

> The sun, the planets and the earth are all objects capable of investigation by the same methods of observation; they are equally objects of sense-perception. God and the religions are not objects in the same class... God is not accessible to observation in the same sense in which the world religions are, and we have no frame of reference within which we can compare God as He really is with God conceived in the world religions... What claims to be a model for the unity of religions turns out in fact to be the claim that one theologian's conception of God is the reality which is the central essence of all religions.[5]

Newbigin further argues that Hick's position is one of ultimate commitment to the God of Philosophical Idealism, and that his confession of a Transcendent Being infinitely greater than is known in all religions is as much a confessional starting point as Newbigin's confession that Jesus Christ is Lord. And he adds:

> Every attempt to form a coherent understanding of the whole human situation starts from an initial act of faith. There is no possibility of knowing anything except on the basis of something which is, at least provisionally, taken for granted. In this respect the Christian believer and the idealist philosopher share the same human predicament.

Newbigin concludes that he "cannot agree that the position of final authority can be taken by anything other than the gospel — either by a philosophical system or by mystical experience or by the requirements of national and global unity". Nor can he agree that the revelation given in

Jesus can be considered as "one of a type or as requiring interpretation by means of categories based on other ways of understanding the totality of experience".

In spite of the use of words like "provisionally" and "final", this seems to suggest that a person's faith may be affirmed as final or ultimate authority in isolation from relatively valid penultimate concerns inherent in rationality, spirituality and community. That impression is not adequately corrected by Newbigin's affirmation that the ultimacy of the confession of Christ does not mean that Christians are not open to adherents of other faith-commitments, that Christians will want to "share in our common patrimony as human beings made by the One God in His own image", and that it may even call into question "much of the intellectual construction, the piety, the practice", etc. of the expressions of one's faith.

Hick takes up the debate in his essay "Belief and Inter-faith Dialogue".[6] He points out that the adherents of Christianity, Islam, Hinduism and Marxism coming together in confessional dialogue will learn about their respective convictions and compare them, but "insofar as they hold to the absolute truth of their own traditions each will be basically concerned to try to bring the others to share his own faith"; so that the dialogue will consist "basically in the display and comparison of their incompatible beliefs". He grants that the distinction which confessionalists make between the phenomenon of Christianity and commitment to Jesus Christ has a certain openness in it and could be fruitful. But he adds that among the intellectual constructions which may have to be changed are the doctrines of the incarnation and the Trinity. This amounts to demanding the rejection not just of some intellectual beliefs but of the very faith-commitment to Jesus Christ as the revelation of the Ultimate as the condition of dialogue in search of truth and community. In fact, Hick demands that the search start without any faith-commitment, Christian or any other, assuming of course that this demand itself presupposes no faith-commitment. This is virtually denying the basic character of the nature of religious faith, namely that it involves the commitment of one's whole self to a transcendent or ultimate reality. Newbigin does accept that the Christian partner in dialogue will inevitably put his or her Christianity at risk; one "must be ready to face the possibility of radical reconsideration of long-accepted formulations". "But", he adds, "he does so within his ultimate commitment to Jesus Christ as finally determinative of his way of understanding and responding to all experience."[7]

The relation between the ultimate and the penultimate dimensions of the human being in historical existence is dialectical. I have no doubt that

Newbigin is right in maintaining that everyone has a faith-commitment underlying the rational, moral, social and other pursuits, and truth is best served by recognizing it and openly avowing it. But every faith-commitment must reckon with the penultimate commitments or concerns of the common humanity which we share with others. The ultimate is present in the midst of the penultimates; and digging into the nature of penultimate human goals we may discover that they have their ground in a transcendent ultimate, which/who is an Other. There can be no confession of the ultimate faith except in the language of the penultimate; and if the forms of that confession are put at risk, in a sense it is faith itself that is risked. Therefore one could say that within the ultimate faith-commitment, commitment to the rational, the moral, the social and other common goals has its legitimacy and its relative autonomy; and further, that this relative autonomy includes even testing people's faith-commitments in the light of these categories, without claiming ultimacy for the test. But we should expect in this process new light to be shed on our ultimate commitments.

Theology is not just the explication of our faith in Jesus Christ. It involves also putting that faith alongside other faiths, and alongside rationality and other human values which we share with others, allowing the examination of each, including our faith, in the categories of the others. In this process we, as Christians, risk Christ for Christ's sake. But we also hope to show that rationality, morality, community and other values require grounding in the faith-dimension, and to reaffirm our confession of the ultimacy of Christ as the judge and redeemer of human rationality, community and other penultimate values — as well as of the religiosity of humankind.

Living faiths and their interaction

Let us begin with a phenomenological survey of religion, religious pluralism and the history of inter-religious relations in modern history. In so doing, one has to see Christianity as "one of a type". Of course, it is widely recognized today even by the natural scientists that all typology and classification in the sciences represent a rational attempt to make sense of complex realities, and should not be pressed to the extent of denying uniqueness to individual phenomena or of affirming that the general conclusions or laws deduced from such typology constitute objective truth. One should be specially cautious of this in the study of religions. Nevertheless, it is a necessary exercise, a necessary basis for any theological reflection.

First, what does it mean to say that human beings, both as individuals and as people, have a spiritual nature? Humankind has evolved from sub-human nature which lives by the laws of natural necessity, and remains part of the organic nature which obeys the evolutionary principle of adaptation to environment. Biblically too, the human being is taken from the dust of the earth. But what distinguishes human beings from animals and other sub-human creatures is that they are aware of being part of nature, and in that way have become aware of a selfhood that transcends nature, stands over against nature as an-other, and feels called upon to transform it and use it for purposes transcending natural necessity. It is this sense of self, with its awareness of being involved in and limited by the necessities of nature and of the freedom to conceive purposes beyond them and to subordinate natural necessities to self-chosen purposes, which constitutes the spiritual nature of humanity.

This realm of finite freedom and self-determination immediately raises at the centre of the human self the question of an ultimate purpose or destiny and of a realm of ultimate reality which is infinite. Thus the awareness of the self is accompanied not only by the sense of the world; there is also the sense of being encountered by the realm of the Infinite or the Holy. It is this that makes for religious consciousness. Humanity is this Self-World-God complex. The self's relation to the world which constitutes a people's culture is set within some "structure of meaning and sacredness" to which people are committed, convinced as they are that it constitutes in some sense their ultimate destiny.

It is of course possible for a people to build a culture on the basis that the world is illusion or that God is illusion, but all peoples have to deal with the trio of self, world and God in some way. Those who consider the world as ultimately illusory still have to build their relation with the world and their patterns of social living, while seeking their destiny of spiritual liberation from the illusory world. And materialists who deny God must find meaning and sacredness within the complex of their relation with the world of nature and society. Human spirituality may also work out a relation of the self with the world considering both as relative realities under God.

So we come to the nature of religion. The core of any religion is the nature of the response of the people to the pressure of the Ultimate Reality on their spirit. The initiative remains with the transcendent Holy, the Truth that makes itself known at the centre of human selfhood. The response to that is self-commitment, in fear and trembling, to what or who is visualized as the Truth or the Holy God. Depending on the self's orientation, the visualization of the Universal Divine varies. And though self-commitment is universal to all religious consciousness, its nature varies. Since love involves self-determination and responsible decision, the human response to the divine vision which is the core of faith in any religious tradition could be true to reality, involve distortions or even a denial of that reality. But that faith-core is fundamental in understanding the religious tradition of a people. It must be added that we speak here of a corporate phenomenon. The faith thus understood is the transcendent spiritual centre of a religion. But as it gives ultimate meaning to human existence the central spiritual faith-response has to find expression in the life of the people.

Paul D. Devanandan speaks of three expressions of the transcendent faith-core in any religious tradition: creed, cultus and culture.[8] Historians of religion have proved that cultus, that is, rites of religious worship and sacraments, and culture — the pattern of relating human beings to nature, society and cosmos — have primacy in the religious life of any people.[9] But the human person being rational, cultus and culture are accompanied, except in the traditional religions and the primal stages of other religions, by attempts to give intellectual formulation of the faith in creeds, doctrinal concepts and philosophies. In fact it is the cultic and credal expressions of the core faith which today we call "religion". But the basic framework of a people's culture, involving the distinctive ethos and ethics or value-system for building patterns of relations with nature and with one another in society, has also been integral to religion. Thus we may say that in every religious tradition there has been an integration of faith, religion (cultus and creed) and culture, forming a total complex.

Looking at human history as a whole, which we are able to do today, we can see a number of religious complex totalities of this kind. History of religions uses several typologies to understand them. Söderblom, Otto and Zahner speak of the "mystic" and "prophetic" types. Others speak of them as monistic and monotheistic (Richard Niebuhr), ontocratic and theocratic (van Leeuwen), religions of tranquillity and anxiety (Arapura). In my book *Man and the Universe of Faiths*[10] I have identified them as Unitive and Messianic to distinguish their concept of history — in the one case cyclic and in the other moving towards a goal. The real difference lies in the conception of the Ultimate Divine and its relation to the world of phenomena and history.

The mystic type of religions sees the Ultimate as the undifferentiated unity of the Spirit or the Absolute, behind or before the diversity and disunity in the phenomenal world. Here human destiny lies in the liberation of the human spirit from the particularity of the self and of the many to become part of the one Universal Self.

To be sure, there are varieties of mystic religions. Indeed there is a great deal to be said for the theory that all the peoples of the world started with cosmic religions which express a "primal vision" of the totality in which the spirits animating nature, human beings and their ancestors and the gods are seen as extensions of an undifferentiated unity. This type of mystic faith is characteristic of the religion of tribal and village peoples in most societies, and perhaps forms the sub-structure of all the other religious traditions. It may perhaps be considered as forming the fundamental spirituality and world-view of traditional Africa. Since the cosmic religious vision does not differentiate between religion, culture and society, or between priest, king and prophet, and is largely lacking in organization, peoples committed to this vision have been unable to withstand the onslaughts of the more organized missionary religions like Islam and Christianity. But converts are often seen to continue to cling to the cosmic spirituality and world-view held in some relation to the new religions they have embraced.

Self-realization through the unitive spiritual experience of the One manifested in the Many, the One behind the Many, or the One without the Many, has been the fundamental goal of liberation in the religions of Indian origin, and they have developed metaphysics and yogic discipline to support the seeker. Hinduism, with its philosophy of the Transcendent Absolute Being, gave rise to Buddhism, with its spiritual Absolute of Non-Being which has taken many forms in the various Asian countries. Taoism in China also belongs to the same mystic type. With the Ultimate seen as Formless Spirit, mystic religions see all forms of popular religion and all gods as belonging to the realm of spiritual immaturity, and they are tolerated only as relative paths leading to the unitive vision. The social and historical realms of human existence have no ultimate spiritual significance, but are spiritually sanctioned as empirical reality.

In contrast to the mystic type of religions, the prophetic type sees the ultimate reality as personal, creating the world for a righteous end and revealing God's law and purpose to humankind, through prophets and through the mighty acts of God, to bring history to its appointed end. Here faith-response consists in human beings sharing the revealed purpose of God and belonging to the prophetic/messianic community obeying the will of God. Judaism, and in some sense Zoroastrianism, are prototypes of this. From within the Jewish spiritual tradition have emerged the religions of Christianity and Islam.

The secular faiths of the modern period are also products of the prophetic religious tradition. Rejecting God as illusion, they affirm the reality of a purpose working itself out in human history through the mighty acts of humankind. Thus we have Liberal Humanism with its notion of inevitable evolutionary progress through the messianism of the rational individual, Communism with its idea of the inevitable revolutionary dialectical progress through the messianism of the proletariat class, and Fascism with the belief in historical fulfilment through world domination by the people of a particular nation or race.

Liberalism, Communism and Fascism are in fact secular ideologies which emerged in modern Western cultural history, and they are in revolt against anything beyond the secular. They demanded ultimate commitment first from individuals and later from whole peoples. Defining "religion" as the realm of the human being's "ultimate concern", Paul Tillich includes them within the world of religious pluralism.[11] He distinguishes them from the traditional religions by describing them as "quasi-religions". Some have called them "pseudo-religions". It may be better however to consider them as secular faiths to distinguish them from religious faiths, faith-commitment being common to all of them.

Of course traditional religious faiths also have had their laws and principles giving direction to people in the patterning of secular life, and many religious believers today combine their religious faith with a relative commitment to some secular ideology or other to define their approach to social and political action. In such cases the secular ideologies are not "quasi-religions" (in the Tillichian sense) or secular faiths. It is only when the secular realm is given ultimacy and the loyalty of the human self to an ideology becomes total that secularism becomes "closed" and takes on that faith character.

This understanding of religious/secular faiths as total complexes, each with its own core of faith-apprehension of the ultimate reality and the meaning of human existence, strengthens the position that no faith can finally interpret other faiths except from its own dogmatic core. This point was made strongly by Hans Küng in an address he gave on "The Christian Revelation and World Religions":

> We confess from the very start that we are trying to answer this question (of religions) from the *Christian* standpoint. No one has a right to describe this in advance as intolerant and exclusive. It may indeed be described as a "dogmatic" standpoint. But on this, it should simply be said that in this sense the non-Christian religions also proceed from a "dogmatic" or "absolute" standpoint... The type of religion which first appeared in Greece and has been particularly

> successful in modern times in the form of the *Enlightenment* is essentially *dogmatic*... erecting *rational*, "*scientific*" *knowledge* into an absolute... But the religions... taking the form of "mysticism" to which the myths are merely symbols... while it is the *inner formless mystical experience of the divine* which is made into an absolute (e.g. Radhakrishnan)... It is only possible to make all religions *equal* if the underlying formless mystical experience is being set up as an *absolute*... As against the religions of enlightenment and the religions of mysticism, then, Christianity considered simply in terms of phenomenology of religion appears as a way whose starting point is neither more nor less dogmatic than that of other religions.[12]

Thus the pluralism of faiths in our day may be considered as consisting of four types — faiths of the primal vision, the Eastern mystic religions, the messianic religious faiths and the messianic secular faiths. All the four types of spirituality can of course be found in all these broad traditions. The primal world-view, as has already been stated, is present universally as the substratum of all religious and secular faiths. Jewish, Christian and Islamic religions have had their continuous tradition of mystics and mysticisms, though the mystic vision has not been recognized as the centre of these religions, and not infrequently mysticisms of the monistic type were even excluded as heresies. Similarly Hinduism, Buddhism and Taoism have developed panentheistic and theistic streams, which have even been affirmed sometimes as the main streams. We can only use a typology to understand the plurality, we cannot overdo it. My main purpose in drawing attention to this phenomenological classification is only to indicate certain trends in the history of interfaith meetings and encounters in the modern period.

Let us now look at the interaction between the various faiths.

Firstly, while traditionally the totality of every religion has been an integration of core-faith, credal and cultic expressions and cultural patterns reflecting the core-faith, the cultural element everywhere is in various stages of breaking up. The Christendom pattern of a religiously Christian culture in the West was broken up by the Renaissance, the Reformation and the Enlightenment and the process of secularization they brought about. The impact of the mixed Christian and secular culture of the West on non-Western non-Christian cultures undermined their traditional religion-culture integration. The secular technological culture has its impact in all parts of the world. While it would be wrong to say that traditional religions no longer influence cultural patterns, it can be affirmed that the interaction between peoples and religions has led to the greatest transformations and interpenetrations at the level of culture.

These changes are represented by the word "modernization"; it indicates the ferment created in every culture by the introduction of science and science-based technology and the cultural values associated with them, and the attempts of religiously pluralistic societies to build national communities on new value systems and social ideals.

In the nineteenth century, when the secular culture was spreading throughout the world and it was generally believed that a higher quality of material, social and human existence would gradually be realized, the mystic religions of Asia and the primal religions of Africa sought not only to assimilate the new cultural values but also to reinterpret their own creeds and cultus, and even their faith-core, to provide a religious and spiritual foundation for cultural modernization. In this process, the Asian and African peoples sought to absorb into their faith framework as much of the prophetic type of religiosity as was possible. Of course some of them were "converted" to secular humanistic faiths or to Christianity as they sought a spiritual foundation for the development of their peoples, and to come to terms with the sense of historical mission which has accompanied the national awakening of the peoples of the non-Western world. As the messianic faiths were seen as the spiritual wave of the future of humankind, the mystic faiths and the peoples of the mystic tradition sought to enter into the "theological" and "anthropological" circle of messianism.

However, the world tragedies of the twentieth century halted this move of the primal and Eastern religions into the messianic spiritual circle. Two world wars, the emergence of Hitlerism and Stalinism, the threat of nuclear annihilation, increasing poverty among two-thirds of the world population — all these have put a question mark on the secular Western culture and the secular and religious faith traditions behind it. So there has been a reverse process in more recent years. Adherents of secular humanistic messianisms have been seeking some religious faith which can tolerate and help them live with the tragic vision of human existence. And even adherents of the messianic religious tradition are seen to search for a cosmic unitive spiritual vision either of the primal or Eastern variety, and its cyclic concept of history which would enable them to accept "the terror of history".

Mircea Eliade put this as follows:

> From the nineteenth century on, linear and the progressive conceptions of history assert themselves more and more, inaugurating faith in an infinite progress, a faith already proclaimed by Leibniz, predominant in the century of

> the Enlightenment and popularized in the nineteenth century by the triumph of the idea of the evolutionists. We must wait until over our own century to see the beginnings of certain new reactions against this historical linearism and a certain revival of interest in the theory of cycles; so it is that, in political economy, we are witnessing the rehabilitation of the notions of cycles, fluctuation, periodic oscillation; that in philosophy the myth of eternal return is revivified by Nietzche; or that in the philosophy of history a Spengler or a Toynbee concern themselves with the problem of periodicity.[13]

The Jewish theologian Richard Rubenstein, in his agonizing attempts to understand Hitlerism and the death-camps in the heart of Europe, sees the messianic tradition of the Bible and the Judeo-Christian civilization as the real culprit. He wants the Jewish people to move away from the God of history to the gods of nature, especially in the new state of Israel:

> Once again, we have come in contact with those powers of life and death, which engendered men's feelings about Baal, Astarte and Anath. These powers have again become decisive in our religious life.[14]

This is the significance of the movements of counter-culture and the popularity in countries like the USA of new cults like Hare Krishna.

This reverse move in the West from the messianic to the mystic apprehension of reality has also brought to the secularized or Westernized Africans and Asians a new self-consciousness regarding the need to explore at depth their cosmic or mystic spiritual traditions and their faith-cores.

Thus our pluralistic situation is marked by two contradictory trends. On the one hand, the pressure of modernization pushes all primal and mystic traditions in the direction of accommodating messianic religious spirituality and secular culture within them, or of converting to messianic religions or secular faiths. On the other, in grappling with the tragic realities of dehumanization and the threat to the future brought about by modern historical dynamism, there is not only a tendency on the part of messianic and ideological faiths to turn away from secular to religious faiths, but even a move to accommodate the unitive vision more fully within them, or for their adherents to be converted to primal or mystic faiths. This is what makes spiritual dialogue between faiths an intra-reality in all traditions.

It is significant that in the report of the Nairobi Assembly of the WCC on the "Search for Community in a Pluralistic Age", this fact is recognized:

In the last few centuries a new situation has arisen. The gospel has been made known all over the world and people of various faiths and convictions have been faced with the person and teaching of Jesus Christ. This has worked as a ferment widely outside the borders of the Christian community and in that sense Christ's work is not confined to the limits of the Church.

At this point our Hindu guest drew attention to the fact that while it is true that Jesus Christ has worked as a ferment among the people of other faiths, it is also true that insights from such religions as Hinduism and Buddhism, etc., are working as a ferment among some Christians and others in Europe, the USA and elsewhere.[15]

Towards a new theology of interfaith dialogue

The ecumenical movement, represented by post-Vatican II Catholicism and the World Council of Churches, recognizes this historical situation of religious and ideological pluralism as a new stage in human history. It is also aware that the new situation calls for a new Christological understanding of our common humanity, with all its secular and religious dimensions, and also of the life and mission of the church in relation to those of other religious and secular ideological communities of faith in God's scheme of salvation consummating in God's kingdom.

The Vatican II document on the "Church Today" begins by recognizing that the human race is passing through a new stage in its history, and that, therefore, the church has the "duty of scrutinizing the signs of the times and of interpreting them in the light of the gospel" before it can clarify not only to Christians but to the whole humanity "how it conceives the presence and activity of the church in the world today". One of the most important features of the times is described thus:

> Today's spiritual agitation and the changing conditions of life are part of a broader and deeper revolution... This scientific spirit exerts a new kind of impact on the cultural sphere and on modes of thought. Technology is now transforming the face of the earth and is already trying to master outer space. To a certain extent the human intellect is also broadening its dominion over time: over the past by means of historical knowledge; over the future by the art of projecting and by planning.

The document goes on to point out that modernity has brought about a certain kind of unity of humankind and of interdependence of peoples: "The destiny of the human community has become all of a piece, where once various groups of men had a kind of private history of their own. Thus the human race has passed from a rather static concept of reality to a more dynamic evolutionary one." But it has brought an ideological pluralism, with deep ideological rivalries, enhancing the peril of war and mutual destruction: "Although the world of today has a very vivid sense of its unity and how one man depends on another in needful solidarity, it is most grievously torn into opposing camps by conflicting forces... True, there is a growing exchange of ideas but the very words by which key concepts are expressed take on quite different meanings in diverse ideological systems."

The unity we have needs to be reinforced through an emphasis on spiritual unity. But we confront a deep spiritual crisis. It is this crisis which makes it necessary to consider the question of religious pluralism in a new light.[16] The "Declaration on the Relationship of the Church to Non-Christian Religions" states:

> In our times, when every day men are being drawn closer together and the ties between the various people are being multiplied, the Church is giving deeper study to the relationship with non-Christian religions... In her task of fostering unity and love among men, and even among nations, she gives primary consideration in this document to what human beings have in common and to what promotes fellowship among them.

The World Council of Churches' new approach to community in a world of religious and ideological pluralism is based on the same considerations, as is clear from the Nairobi Assembly report on "The Common Search of People of Various Faiths, Cultures and Ideologies":

> Our generation has become keenly aware of the religious plurality of the world... This plurality is augmented and criss-crossed by further differences... between ideologies and cultures...
>
> But there is more than a new and sharper awareness of other faiths and communities of faith. There is a great urgency for seeking a community beyond our own. Whether we like it or not, we find ourselves thrown in with all of humanity in a common concern for justice and peace. We have been thrown together in an interdependent world, in which the urgency is that of survival or extinction.
>
> In that world we cannot allow our faith, the gift of our sense of community in Jesus Christ, to add to the tensions and suspicions and hatreds that threaten to tear apart the one family of humanity. We cannot allow our faith to be abused for such demonic purposes. We must seek the wider community without compromising the true *skandalon* of the gospel.[17]

What then is the theological basis of the search for this "wider community" of all humanity? What is the relation of the church, the community which acknowledges God as revealed in Jesus Christ, to this wider community?

Here we have of course had the traditional approaches in terms of the relation between Creation and Redemption — in the Catholic tradition as imperfect Nature perfected in Grace; in the Protestant as fallen Nature destroyed by divine wrath and recreated by Grace through faith; and in the Orthodox tradition as the Spirit active in creation and in the church. But such theological formulations in the past had taken place within a static view of reality which is no more acceptable. Today they need reformulation and development. As long as the realm of redemptive Grace is considered the same as the visible church, there can be no adequate theological basis for a common search with other religions and ideologies to achieve this wider human community.

The Nairobi Assembly report says: "Some seem to be called to bold pioneering, adventures and risks beyond the confines of present ecclesiastical and theological structures. Others acknowledge an equally exacting calling to deepen the time-honoured understanding of the community that is ours in Christ."[18]

Theologians like John Hick follow the former path. We are concerned here with the efforts of the latter group, within the ecumenical movement, to deepen the traditional understanding of Christ and fellowship-in-Christ in a more inclusive way. The concern for continuity with traditional theologies brings out the confessional tensions in the starting points. Nevertheless, the move beyond them, especially in dialogue with theologies emerging from traditionally pluralistic societies like India, brings new elements into the picture and presents us with new insights.

That is why I attempt in the following pages to deal with the contributions, in the area of the theology of religion, of two Indian theologians, Raymond Panikkar and Paul Devanandan, and to do so in the context of the ferment in the ecumenical movement in general.

NOTES

[1] *The Meaning and End of Religion*, New York, Macmillan, 1963.
[2] London, Duckworth, 1975.
[3] In *World Faiths*, No. 103, autumn 1977, pp.2-19.
[4] New York, St Martin's, 1973, p.131.
[5] *The Open Secret: Sketches for a Missionary Theology*, Grand Rapids, Eerdmans, 1978, pp.181-191 (for this and the following two quotations).
[6] In *God Has Many Names*, Philadelphia, Westminster Press, pp.116-124.

[7] *Open Secret, op. cit.*, pp.209-210.
[8] *Christian Concern in Hinduism*, Bangalore, CISRS, 1961, p.10.
[9] Cf. W.C. Smith, *Faith and Belief*, Princeton, Princeton University Press, 1979.
[10] Madras, CLS, 1975.
[11] *Christianity and the Encounter of the World Religions*, New York and London, Columbia University Press, 1963.
[12] In J. Neuner ed., *Christian Revelation and World Religions*, London, Burns & Oates, 1967, pp.47-50.
[13] *Cosmos and History: the Myth of the Eternal Return*, New York, Harper, 1959, pp.145-146.
[14] *After Auschwitz: Radical Theology and Contemporary Judaism*, Indianapolis, Bobber-merril, p.70.
[15] *Breaking Barriers: Nairobi 1975*, ed. David Paton, London, SPCK, and Grand Rapids, Wm B. Eerdmans, 1976, p.77.
[16] "The Church Today", paras 4 & 5, from *Documents of Vatican II*, ed. Walter Abbot, New York, Herder & Herder and Association Press, 1966.
[17] *Breaking Barriers, op. cit.*, p.74.
[18] *Ibid.*, pp.74-75.

2. Towards "an Ecumenical Ecumenism"

A. DEVELOPMENTS IN CATHOLIC THOUGHT

Vatican II and post-Vatican II discussions

The traditional position of the Roman Catholic Church is summed up in the assertion: "Outside the church no salvation." Consistent with the theological distinction between the natural and supernatural dimensions of the human being, Catholic theology has always maintained that the human being lost through sin only the supernatural grace and that, while the natural is imperfect without the supernatural, nature retains elements of divine goodness and knowledge. Therefore it has recognized the existence of a natural knowledge of God among human beings, expressing itself in "natural religions". The Roman Catholic Church has also maintained the possibility of persons who have never heard the gospel attaining divine salvation through their obedience to the dictates of conscience. The Vatican's condemnation in 1949 of Fr Feeney's view that there is no saving grace working outside the historical Catholic Church illustrates this traditional position.[1] Within it, however, the question of the salvific value of other religions as such had never been raised. It is the raising of this question which is new in the major theological trends initiated in this area by Vatican II.

The main contribution of Vatican II to the theology of pluralism lies in its recognition (1) that human beings are not just individuals but persons-in-relation to the historical religious or atheistic communities in which they live, and (2) that the salvific will of God, that is, the operation of saving grace, is universal, embracing all humanity.

From these premises the following insights emerge: All peoples have the possibility, open to them in their own situations, to partake in the paschal mystery of Jesus Christ, and this participation is realized often in inscrutable ways. All peoples are thus related to the church, the people of

Christ, as near or distant relations. Therefore the church should see itself as "the universal sacrament of salvation", pointing to and fulfilling the positive value of the spiritual search for God in other religions and for fullness of life in community among secular atheists.

Let us take a brief look at some of the Vatican II documents.

The *Dogmatic Constitution of the Church* begins with the self-understanding of the church as the universal sacrament of human salvation: "By her relationship with Christ the Church is a kind of sacrament or sign of man's intimate union with God and of the unity of mankind." It is also "the instrument for the achievement of such union and unity".

"All men are called to be part of this Catholic unity of the people of God"; in fact they all "belong to it or are related to it in various ways, the Catholic faithful as well as all who believe in Christ, and indeed the whole of mankind; for all men are called to salvation by the grace of God." Even outside any knowledge of the church or of Jesus Christ, or even of God, the Holy Spirit grants to people faith and the reality of salvation:

> Nor is God far distant from those who in shadows and images seek the unknown God; for He gives all men life and breath and all things (cf. Acts 17:25-58) and as Saviour wants all men to be saved (cf. Tim. 2:4). Those who through no fault of theirs are still ignorant of the Gospel of Christ and His Church, yet sincerely seek God and with the help of divine Grace strive to do His will as known to them through the voice of conscience, those men can attain the eternal salvation. Nor does divine providence deny the assistance necessary to salvation to those who, without having attained, through no fault of their own, to an explicit knowledge of God, are striving, not without divine Grace, to lead a good life.

The *Pastoral Constitution on the Church in the Modern World* brings out most clearly the universality of the paschal mystery of Christ and the possibility of participation in it, open to all people irrespective of their religious faith or even lack of it.

In fact this document takes up the issue of Christian dialogue with modern atheism. Since "the word atheism is applied to phenomena which are quite distinct from one another" it clearly distinguishes the different types of atheism. "Undeniably those who wilfully shut out God" against the dictates of their conscience are "not free from blame". But a good deal of atheism is simply the erroneous intellectual climate in which science, philosophy and social humanism pursue rational truths or affirm human rights. Scientism "transgresses the limits of the positive sciences". Some humanists "seem more inclined to affirm man than to deny God". Indeed many reject "fallacious" ideas of God and not the "God of the Gospel".

Atheism also arises from "a violent protest against evil in the world" and by raising "certain human values" to the stature of God. Atheism gets systematized when God and religion are seen as obstacles to human freedom or the struggle for social liberation.

The document admits that Christianity itself must "bear some responsibility for this situation", for it is in "critical reaction" against the deficiencies of "the religious, moral or social life" of Christianity that sometimes atheism emerged as the climate for modern science and society. The church should become conscious of the weighty questions which atheism raises and examine them seriously. The church's attitude to atheists is described as dialogical partnership in and for community.

> While rejecting atheism root and branch, the Church sincerely professes that all men, believers and unbelievers alike, ought to work for the rightful betterment of this world, in which all alike live. Such an ideal cannot be realized however apart from sincere and prudent dialogue.

It is almost as a theological response to this atheistic framework within which many in the modern world work for a fuller human life that the document presents Jesus Christ as "the New Man" in whom "all the aforementioned truths find their root and attain their crown". In him humanity is born anew. "He blazed a new trail", and in his death and resurrection "life and death are made holy and take on a new meaning." This is true for Christian believers. It is also true "for all men of good will".

> All this holds true not only for Christians but for all men of good will in whose hearts grace works in an unseen way. For since Christ died for all men, and since the ultimate vocation of man is in fact one and divine, we ought to believe that the Holy Spirit, in a manner known only to God, offers to every man the possibility of being associated with this paschal mystery.

According to the *Document on Mission*, while wilful rejection of the gospel and the church leads people to perdition, "God in ways known to Himself can lead those inculpably ignorant of the gospel to that faith without which it is impossible to please Him" (Heb. 11:6).

Vatican II sees a positive relation between the grace of God at work universally and the religions of humanity. According to the mission document, "the universal design of God for the salvation of the human race is not carried out exclusively in the soul of a man", but includes the world of concrete historical religions which is the realm of humanity's "search for God, groping for Him that they may by chance find Him" (cf. Acts 17:27). Under Divine Providence these religions "may sometimes serve as a guidance course towards the true God or as a preparation of the gospel". And whatever truth and grace and treasures God has distributed among the nations are "a sort of secret presence of God"; and anything of value present "in the rites and cultures" of various peoples is "healed, ennobled and perfected for the glory of God" in the church by the illumination of the gospel. In the decree on the church also it is affirmed that "whatever good is latent in the religious practices and cultures of diverse peoples" is redeemed and perfected.

The *Declaration on Non-Christian Religions* states that whatever is "true and holy" in the non-Christian religions reflects "a ray of that Truth which enlightens all men" and is revealed in Christ. In him and in his church God offers "the fullness of religious life" to all humanity and "reconciliation of all things to himself" (cf. 2 Cor. 5:18-19).

That is why Vatican II seeks to arrange the peoples of the various concrete religious traditions of humankind in concentric circles with the Catholic Church at the centre. It is significant that these circles embrace non-Catholic Christians, peoples following other religions — and even atheists, though only as a distant relative.

> — the church recognizes that in many ways she is united with those who, being baptised, are honoured with the name of Christian;
> — finally those who have not yet received the Gospel are related in various ways to the people of God. In the first place there is the people to whom the covenants and the promises were given and from whom Christ was born according to the flesh (cf. Rom. 9:4-5; 11:28-29).
>
> But the plan of salvation also includes those who acknowledge the Creator. In the first place among these are the Moslems... Nor is God Himself far distant from those who in shadows and images seek the unknown God... Nor does divine providence deny the help necessary for salvation to those who... have not attained at an explicit knowledge of God but who strive to live a good life thanks to His grace.[2]

"Anonymous Christianity"

Among the theologians who have worked out their theology of the salvific value of non-Christian religions, Karl Rahner, H.R. Schlette and Hans Küng are the foremost.

Karl Rahner's theory of "anonymous Christians" is now well-known. Formulated in the early sixties,[3] Rahner developed it further in his book *Foundations of Christian Faith*[4] in the light of Vatican II. Rahner writes as a dogmatic theologian standing squarely within the framework of the teachings of the Roman Catholic Church.

Rahner recognizes that inter-religious relations are entering a new phase in the modern world-setting, and that it is necessary to re-examine the Catholic relation to non-Christian religions from the dogmatic self-understanding of Catholic Christianity as "the absolute religion", i.e. as the religion which is "objectively" the destiny of all humankind and therefore demanding "absolute subjective obligation" from anyone since it challenges him or her spiritually as the truth of human existence. From that historical moment when Christianity presents itself to the conscience as one's spiritual destiny, one has "no salvation outside the Church", and from then on no other religion can have any salvific value for him or her. The question, however, is whether other religions have a place till that time, that is in humanity's "pre-Christian history", understood not chronologically as before Jesus Christ's coming but existentially as before Jesus Christ's coming to the particular person or people. Rahner's answer is *Yes*.

Firstly, because of the universal salvific will of God as revealed in Jesus Christ (1 Tim. 2:4). This means that God must provide the means for the salvation of all people at all times. Therefore the Holy Spirit must provide sinful humanity not only with natural knowledge of God but also with supernatural knowledge of God's grace. Secondly, because human salvation cannot just be a matter of the inner spirit of an individual; it must be mediated and realized through and in concrete historical socio-religious tradition. It means that God must provide the means of saving grace in the pre-Christian history of human persons and peoples in the religions in which they are born and brought up.

For these reasons, then, non-Christian religions are means of salvation for men and women who have not been existentially challenged by the gospel of Christ.

Further, Catholic theology acknowledges that Christ alone saves, and therefore wherever saving grace occurs it is through Jesus Christ. Even before the manifestation of God's redeeming grace in the Jesus of history, the Holy Spirit who makes universal provision for means of grace in other religions "can be called the Spirit of *Jesus Christ*". Rahner explains it thus: "In so far as the universal efficacy of the Spirit is always oriented towards the high point of the historical mediation, it can truly be said that this Spirit is everywhere and from the outset the spirit of *Jesus Christ*, the logos of God who became man."[5] Dogmatically speaking non-Christian religions must manifest in their history what Rahner calls "a searching memory" which is "directed" towards the coming event of the absolute Saviour "in hope and in anticipation".[6]

If men and women saved through other religions are saved by Jesus Christ, it is "permissible", says Rahner, to "confront" an adherent of a non-Christian religion not as a mere *non*-Christian but as "someone who can and must already be regarded in this or that respect as an anonymous Christian". This will also mean interpreting non-Christian religions as "Christianity of an anonymous kind".

This approach to other religions as legitimate pre-Christian means of human salvation, in turn, calls for a change in the self-understanding of the church and its worldwide mission. The church cannot any more consider itself as "the exclusive community" of the saved over against the lost communities outside the church. Rather, the church is the "historically tangible vanguard of what the Christian hopes is present as a hidden reality even outside the visible Church". As the communion of those "who can explicitly confess" the name by which all are destined to salvation, the missionary activity of the church is aimed to bring to "explicit consciousness" the hidden Christ and salvation present in these religions.

With the church's mission becoming more effective, the gospel of Jesus Christ will become existentially present to the conscience of more and more people, and the character of non-Christian religions as legitimate pre-Christian means of salvation should gradually disappear. Rahner keeps open the question as to whether some religions will remain so legitimate till the end of time.

In his book *Towards a Theology of Religions*,[7] H.R. Schlette follows much the same approach in working towards a theology of religious pluralism.

The divine covenant with Noah, which embraces the whole of humanity, is the framework within which the covenant with Abraham, and through him with the people of Israel, is made (Gen. 8-12). Schlette points to this protohistory in the Bible as indicating the "theological position in the believing consciousness of Israel" regarding the history of the divine redemption of humankind. Two histories of divine salvation — a "general sacred history" and a "special sacred history" — can be discerned in world history, both expressing the saving will of God, and therefore finding their unity in the End. Schlette sees the religions of humanity as part of the general sacred history and the religion of Israel and the church as forming the special sacred history. Both are willed and sanctioned by God as means of human salvation. The "special" illuminates the meaning of the "general", and both are mediated by Christ and must come together at the end of time. Thus, says Schlette:

> The unity of the human race, God's universal salvific will, the universal redemptive significance of Christ's death and resurrection and the eschatological convergence of all sacred history... belong to the fundamental data of revelation.[8]

Schlette goes on to speak of "the way of non-Christian religions as the ordinary and the way of the Church as the extraordinary way of salvation". Wherein does the distinctiveness of the church consist? It "does not consist of a more advantageous chance of salvation"; but God in his freedom has chosen the church to "reveal his glory before the world" through "a convincing demonstration of his will and action for the salvation of all". Thus the history of the church gives all sacred history its principle of unity and coherence; it is "the few" which represents the destiny of "the many" — "fundamentally, the representation of all by one". It is this representative character of special sacred history which demands that the church must "enquire into the general sacred history which runs parallel to it" if it is to understand its own nature more clearly. This, for him, is the relevance of the Christian theology of non-Christian religions.

Schlette keeps open many questions. For example, the question as to whether "a factual convergence within human history of all religions with Christianity" is part of God's intention. Or the question regarding the role of the non-Christian religions themselves in the conversion of their adherents to explicit faith in Jesus Christ. In his opinion, the transition involved cannot just be "the prolongation of what went before, nor its complete destruction either, but in every case fulfilment as dialectic and dialectic as fulfilment".[9]

Hans Küng, in a speech he gave in Bombay in 1964 on "The World Religions in God's Plan of Salvation", continues the Rahner-Schlette line of thought. He too emphasizes the significance of Gen. 8-12 in Israel's theology of other peoples, and sees the "vast panorama of history within which the covenant idea is preserved in two concentric circles: the Noahite covenant with the whole of humankind and the covenant with Abraham for Israel alone."[10] He traces the two circles in the biblical tradition, both in the Old and New Testaments, and concludes that in the universal plan for the salvation of humankind, "there is no extra, only an intra; no outside, only an inside". He accepts Schlette's description of the non-Christian and Christian ways of salvation as "ordinary" and "extraordinary". Non-Christian religions are "pre-Christian"; directed towards

Christ whom "in their error they do not recognize for what he really is, the Truth". It is Jesus Christ who can liberate the non-Christian religions from their "entanglement in error and sin". Thus Christian faith represents a "radical universalism but one grounded and made concrete in, and united upon, Jesus Christ", and therefore able to avoid "narrow particularism", "indifferentism" for truth, "domination" of one religion or "syncretic mingling which suppresses truth".

The church of Christ in this theological context is "linked" with other religions, called to be in their "midst", "alongside" them and "with" them — "thinking and speaking in solidarity with them", and "serving" them as "the representative of all the people of the world religions", so that "from being Christians *de jure*, they may become Christians *de facto*" by explicit profession in witness.

The Catholic theologians who gathered in Nagpur (India) in 1971 for the Conference on Evangelisation,[11] were in agreement with the basic Rahner/Schlette/Küng approach, though some of them were critical of the use of terms like "anonymous Christians" and "ordinary/extraordinary ways of salvation".

Some emphasized the presence of divine grace in other religions as involving the mediation not only of the Unknown Christ but also of the Latent Church, so as to retain the traditional doctrine of "no salvation outside the church". Elements of a more fundamental criticism emerged at two points.

Firstly, whether the Vatican II and post-Vatican II theologies realistically understood the sinful perversions and errors in other religions; and secondly whether the affirmation that the adherents of other religions are implicitly Christian could be interpreted as meaning that they need not become Christian by profession, or that becoming Christian for them involved no spiritual repentance and conversion, but only a gnostic illumination of what they already are in Christ.

For instance, the Vatican II statement that "whatever goodness found among the non-Christians is a preparation for the gospel" is followed by the warning against those who, deceived by the evil one, are "caught in futile reasoning and have exchanged the truth of God for a lie" (Rom. 1). J. Masson SJ points out that "this stern text was added later despite the objections of those who considered it too harsh". Does it mean that it was not integral to the basic thought of the Council?

Walter Kaspers rejects the Barthian view that religions are idolatrous, but points out the relevance of "the hamartiological aspect" of other religions. He says:

> The teaching of implicit Christianity presupposes on the part of man the openness and readiness of heart to perceive the call of God in the world and to follow it in conscience. However as soon as the *quaestio facti* arises, the judgment of Scripture and tradition does not appear to be very optimistic... (Rom. 1). Consequently, the Old Testament and New Testament, as well as the Church fathers, see in other religions heresy and superstition, lies and deceit, demonic imitation of the true religion, devilish delusions, hybris, the blending of the heart and understanding and moral depravity.[12]

He complains that "this prophetic criticism of religion has to some extent fallen into oblivion and discredit today. It really shouldn't have been. The presentation of the hamartiological aspect necessitates complementing critically the idea of implicit Christianity in non-Christian religion. When one isolates and absolutizes the concept of the Anonymous Christ, then it leads logically to the assertion that Mission has no other concern than 'that the Hindu becomes a better Hindu, the Buddhist a better Buddhist, the Moslem a better Moslem'... The time has come for critical discernment of spirits."[13]

According to James Dupuis SJ: "The Christian revelation does not merely 'unveil' that which remained under a veil in other religions." That would amount to a "Christian gnosticism, to a mere imparting of knowledge". The newness of the Christian religion must be seen as implying "both the full revelation of the mystery and the highest form of its visible mediation and of its presence in the world". Therefore conversion from non-Christian religions to Christianity is "more than a process of explicitation; it is the access to a new order".[14]

With such criticism and certain modifications the consultation of Catholic theologians in 1971 basically accepted the new post-Vatican II approach to non-Christian religions.

A new stage in mission theology

It is within the Catholic Church's mission among non-Christian peoples that theologies of religions have taken definite forms. These have been theologies of mission, justifying the motive and defining the means and goal of the missionary activities of the church. Therefore it is in the history of missions, where the church met the non-Christian peoples to preach to them the gospel of salvation and plant new churches, that we may discern the different stages in the evolving theology of religions.

Aloysius Pieris SJ, a Buddhist scholar and Catholic theologian from Sri Lanka, speaks of the important stages in the history of the Catholic theology of mission to religions.[15] The first stage is represented by

Francis Xavier, missionary to India, China and Japan during the period of Portuguese influence in Asia, when mission was marked by the "Conquest Theory", that is, of contrasting Christianity with other religions in terms of God and the devil, of light and darkness, and therefore of radically displacing other religions by Catholic Christianity. In the effort to save souls, even the use of state power was justified. Then emerged the "Theory of Adaptation". Here too the aim is conquest, but it makes a distinction between religion and culture, enabling the church to adopt and adapt some of the non-religious cultural elements of the non-Christian religions with a view to communicating the gospel in an indigenous manner and building an indigenous Christianity. De Nobili of Tamilnadu (India) and Ricci of China were Western missionaries who represented this attitude to other religions. The Vatican did not at the time approve of the attitude or the policy underlying it. But it finds a prominent place in the Vatican II document on Missions. The more forward-looking Vatican II position is the third, namely the "Fulfilment Theory". Other religions are seen as pre-Christian search for salvation fulfilled in Christianity, or as pre-Christian ways of salvation in Christ finding explicitness and plenitude in the Catholic Church.

Pope Paul's address to representatives of Hinduism, Islam and the Parsee faith during his visit to the Eucharistic Congress in 1964 may be taken as a kind of inauguration of this new theology of mission in Asia. He points to the approach to other religions inherent in the fulfilment theory. That approach involves the recognition of the presence and activity of Christ in the search and experience of God in other religions and a call for a religious dialogue and partnership in building the spiritual foundations of national and global community. The Pope said:

> This visit to India is the culmination of a desire which we have had in mind for a long time. Your land is the house of ancient cultures, the cradle of great religions, the seat of a people which has searched for God with untiring zeal, in deep silence and awe, in hymns of intimate prayer. Seldom is such a holy longing for God marked with words so full of the spirit of the coming of our Lord, as in the words of your holy scriptures, which centuries before Christ beseeched: "Lead me from falsehood to truth; lead me from darkness to light; lead me from death to eternal life." It is a prayer which belongs to our era too. Today more than ever before, this prayer could be uttered from our very own hearts...
>
> Today the human race is experiencing deep-seated changes, and it wavers between basic principles which lead it in life, and between the new forces which will lead it into future life. Even your country has entered a phase in its history in which it is conscious of the insecurity of the present time, when the traditional systems and values are being toppled over. All possible forces must concentrate on building up the future of the nation, not only upon a material

> basis, but upon solid spiritual foundations also... We must therefore stand even closer together, not just via the modern means of communication of the press and the radio, ships and jet-planes, but also through our hearts, through mutual understanding, through reverence and love. We should not meet merely as tourists, but rather as pilgrims who come across each other on the way to their search for God who is to be found not only in stone buildings but in the hearts of men...[16]

To go back to Pieris' historical survey. He goes on to affirm that a fourth theory based on Vatican II, inherent in it but going beyond it, has emerged in the post-Vatican period, namely the Sacramental Theory.

What Vatican II has done is to see the church as not identical with the kingdom of God, but as "an embryonic kingdom in the process of development". Other religions are also brought into relation with the church within the context of the present and future of the kingdom. Pieris here raises a critical question. What does all this mean for the future of Christianity and other religions? To be fulfilled in Christ, will the other religions have to die? What about the church itself? Within the reality of relatedness and communion in Christ, the Christian eucharist, he says, may be interpreted as affirming that "all peoples, even the Hindus, Buddhists and Muslims, by their liturgies and rites, are God's people".

Here the church is seen as the sign and sacrament of the universal Christic salvation realized in the other religions. The strengthening of non-Christians in their own religions is seen as the general aim of Catholic missionary service, not however forgetting the call to some to join the church's special vocation. Buhlmann summarizes this aim as follows:

> In many cases therefore it may suffice for a Hindu to be made a better Hindu, because by doing so he is brought nearer to Christ by whom he is already moved, apart from those cases where the Spirit still requires a Hindu-Christian himself to become the symbol of the kingdom, while he joins the visible Christian community.[17]

B. RAYMOND PANIKKAR: THE UNIVERSAL ONTIC CHRIST

Raymond Panikkar* is a Catholic mystic-philosopher-theologian who has given systematic expression to this movement from the fulfilment

---

* This is not an exhaustive study of Panikkar's thought. We are concentrating on his theology of inter-religious relations. Even on this theme he has written extensively and in several languages. We refer here only to a few of his books in English and some articles in English journals, and our purpose is to indicate the central thrust of his Trinitarian and Christological approach to the relation between Christianity and other religions.

theory to the sacramental. Inheriting the religious traditions of his Spanish Catholic mother and Indian Hindu father, the relation between Christianity and Hinduism has been existentially critical for Panikkar, both spiritually and theologically.

While the first edition of his book *The Unknown Christ of Hinduism*, published in 1964,[18] in general represents the fulfilment theory, in the 1981 revised edition of it the stance is clearly sacramental. The change, while symbolical of his own personal pilgrimage, also corresponds to the radical turn taken by Roman Catholicism within which tradition he stands. In the preface to the 1981 edition he says that as one "at the confluence of the four rivers, the Hindu, Christian, Buddhist and secular traditions", and involved in an "adventure" of relating them to one another, he is seeking to "explain the continuity of my path in spite of the mutation that has taken place both in me and in our world". In fact the starting point in many of his writings is the new theological significance of the pluralistic existence in which we find ourselves. Panikkar, in this context, is seeking "an ecumenical ecumenism", embracing all authentic religious traditions in internal dialogue and interaction, within the framework of a universal Trinity and Christology.

Panikkar's starting points, Trinity and Christ, are confessedly Christian. Of course in dealing with them he goes beyond their traditional categories and meanings by deepening and extending their relevance. To begin thus with the Christian religious tradition is justified, he says, because "the meeting of religions cannot take place on neutral territory, in a no-man's land — which would be a reversion to unsatisfactory individualism and subjectivism. It can take place only at the heart of the religious traditions."[19]

Also, as the traditions have determined the terminology, we have to speak from one or another tradition. Further, "despite development or deepening", Panikkar says, he keeps "a very real continuity" with the church doctrines.

The framework of Trinity

Though Panikkar's exposition of the Trinitarian approach to religious pluralism came after the Christological, it may be as well to start with it as it clarifies the basis of the Christological.

Ewert Cousins of Fordham University, New York, is of the opinion that Panikkar's Trinitarian theology is more systematically worked out than his Christology. He says:

> From the standpoint of his outreach into world religions, I believe that Panikkar should be situated in the vestige tradition of Trinitarian theology. Drawing its classical source from texts in Augustine, this tradition has seen reflections of the Trinity on the material world, the rational soul, interpersonal relations, the Old Testament and Greek philosophy. In this period of global mutation it should not be surprising to see Panikkar extending this tradition into the sphere of mankind's religious experience as this has developed in its highest forms.[20]

The traditional Christian doctrine of Trinity speaks of God as Father, Son and Spirit. Panikkar's *The Trinity and World Religions* is an attempt to interpret the universe of religious and secular faiths within the framework of the threefold spirituality of response to the Trinity of God.

Though the Trinitarian concept of God is metaphysically oriented, Panikkar's emphasis is on spiritual experience, one could even say on mystic *anubhava*. This he shares with the late Swami Abhishiktananda, the French Catholic-Hindu sanyasi of Santhivanam Ashram in India. Abhishiktananda, in his *Hindu-Christian Meeting Point Within the Cave of the Heart*,[21] seeks to interpret the Hindu Advaitic mysticism in terms of the unitive experience of the Trinity of *Sat-Chit-Ananda* and to incorporate it into the Christian mysticism of the Trinity of Father, Son and Spirit. Panikkar had been a member of the "Cuttat group" (so called because of the part J.A. Cuttat, the Catholic Swiss Ambassador to India, played in the group) which was engaged in an enquiry of meditation on the relation between Christian and Advaitic *anubhavas* of God. This enquiry is also the subject of the beautiful little book which Abhishiktananda and Panikkar together wrote on their Christian Hindu pilgrimage to the source of the Ganges, under the title, *The Mountain of the Lord*.[22]

Of *Trinity and World Religions* Panikkar says that it is "far more of a meditation than an erudite study, far more mystical and 'praying' theology than an analytical and cognitive philosophy, though we must refrain from pressing the distinction to the point of dichotomy". This contemplative approach to philosophical theology is typical of Panikkar. Indeed Panikkar thinks that spirituality is the essence of any religion and goes behind its rites, structures and dogmas. The approach to religious pluralism in terms of the presence in religions of common forms of spirituality is therefore important for a dialogue among them.

Panikkar speaks of three forms of spirituality present in the varied religious experiences of humankind. He categorizes them as "action, love and knowledge"; in Hindu terminology as *Karmamarga, Bhaktimarga* and *Jnanamarga*. Elsewhere he speaks of "apophatism, personalism and divine immanence". This threefold spirituality corresponds to the Trinity of God as "Father (Source), Son (Being) and the Spirit (Return of Being)". He quotes Paul's Trinitarian formulation of God "*above* all, *through* all and *in* all" (Eph. 4:6) as providing a clue to this understanding:

— over all, *super omnes*, the source of Being, which is not Being, since if so it would be Being and not its source;
— through all, *per omnia*, the Son, Being and the Christ, he through whom and for whom everything was made, beings being participants in Being;
— within all, *in omnibus*, the Spirit, divine immanence and, in the dynamism of pure act, the end (the return) of Being; for that reason Being — and beings — only exists in so far as it proceeds from its source and continues to flow in the Spirit.

Panikkar's trinity of divinity and spirituality has been summed up by Ewert Cousins as follows: "(1) the Silent apophatic dimension, which he related to the Father, since the Father expresses himself only through the Son and of himself has no word or expressions; (2) the Personalist dimension which Panikkar related to the Son since the Son is personal mediator between God and man, through whom creation, redemption, and glorification flow; and (3) the Immanent dimension which Panikkar relates to the Spirit since Spirit is union of Father and Son."[23]

While the Buddhist experience of *Sunya* (non-being), the Semitic religious experience of the word of God and the Hindu experience of Advaita are illustrations of these three respective spiritualities, all religions according to Panikkar have all the three in some measure, and also have the urge to integrate them. All religions have streams in them militating against a too narrow pursuit of one or another of these spiritualities in isolation. Even atheistic nihilism and humanism are to be interpreted as such protests in religious culture and have a valid role in the emergence of a Trinitarian spirituality in the modern world.

Panikkar uses the classical word *theandrism* for that spirituality in which the divine and the human are united. "Theandrism succeeds in avoiding anthropomorphism on the one hand and theologism on the other. It seeks to re-establish a non-dualistic vision of these two poles of reality which become blurred and vanish when one considers them in isolation, the one from the other. A purely down-to-earth anthropology demotes man, while an exclusively 'revelational' theology destroys God himself."[24] Panikkar sees theandrism as "an authentic synthesis" of the various dimensions of "our life on earth as well as in heaven", a synthesis of "contemplation that is something more than thought" and "action which does not limit its purview to the building of an earthly city", also "a prayer that is not limited to petition or even praise, but also a silence that does not fall into indifference" and "a supernaturalism that is not antinatural" — in short "a sense of the Spirit that is not disincarnate" combined with a sense of the Incarnation that does not neglect the Spirit, an affirmation that is not exclusive and a negation that "is not closed in upon itself". Its anthropology is that "man is more than 'man'; he is a theandric mystery."[25]

Thus Panikkar visualizes the Divine Trinity as "a junction where the authentic spiritual dimensions of all religions meet". And the encounter of religions taking place in the Trinity would result "not in a vague fusion or mutual dilution but in an authentic enhancement of all the religious and even cultural elements that are contained in each".

The universal Christ

Panikkar assumes that the universal salvific will of God is present and active in all religions and that while there is no salvation outside Christ, Christ is at work in all authentic religions through their sacraments:

> Christ is the universal redeemer. There is no redemption apart from him. Where there is no redemption there is no salvation. Therefore any human person who is saved — and we know by reason and by faith that God provides everybody with the necessary means of salvation — is saved by Christ, the only redeemer. This amounts to saying that Christ is present in one form or another in every human being as he journeys towards God.[26]

This means that no religious tradition in which a person journeys towards God can be interpreted as merely "natural", it has to be "fallen or redeemed"; not "simply fallen" because "the mystery of the Cross has a universal efficacy"; but not "simply redeemed" since the effects of redemption may not have been fully accepted or acknowledged. Therefore it is more proper to speak of the relation of other religions to Christ and Christian plenitude in terms of "potency-act, seed-fruit, forerunner-real presence, symbol-reality, desire-accomplishment, allegory-thing-in-itself, and even the specifically Christian dynamism of death and resurrection". In a real sense, Panikkar discerns this as true not only of other religions but also of Christianity. Panikkar's contribution lies in this clarification of the nature of the universal Christ relating Christianity and other religions. He has several theses.

Firstly, Christ is not only the historical Jesus; Christ is more than Jesus, both in form and meaning. This is true even in the traditional Christian doctrine of Christ. In it "he is not only the historical redeemer but also the unique Son of God, the Second Person of the Trinity, the only ontological — temporal and eternal — link between God and the World". Christ as "risen Jesus" is also more than Jesus of Nazareth when the church speaks of "the real presence of Christ in the sacraments" or in "these little ones". If Christ were "a mere reality of the temporal and social order, which existed at a certain time in history and had a certain place in geography, the whole of the Christian faith would collapse".[27] Within the Divine Trinity, God the Son is "the Mystery hidden since the world began". It is through him that everything was made, everything exists, the beginning and the end. Therefore "it is the Son properly speaking — and the Son was manifested in Christ — who is the Divine Person, the Lord". And "Christ — known or unknown" makes religion possible. Even by definition Christ is "the unique link between the created and uncreated, the relative and the absolute, the temporal and the eternal, earth and heaven, the only mediator". Here Christian religion has no monopoly on Christ, nor can Christ's identification with "Jesus only" be presupposed.

> Even from right within Christian faith, such an identification has never been asserted. What the Christian faith does affirm is that Jesus of Nazareth has a special and unique relationship with what Paul, following Old Testament usage, calls the Uncreated Wisdom, what John, following Philo, calls the Logos, and Matthew and Luke, following Judaism, call the Holy Spirit, and what all later tradition has called the Son.[28]

Panikkar says that "the discovery of re-velation of the God-person is a decisive contribution of Christianity"; and Christianity is right in affirming Christic personalism revealed in Jesus as "essential to every evolved attitude". But he would assert (1) that the Divine Trinity includes the Father who is greater than the Son and the Spirit through whom alone interpersonal communion is realized; and (2) that Christ transcends the historical particularism of the Jesus of Nazareth. Therefore the Christ of other religions also represents an extension of the concept of the Universal Christ.

Secondly, every authentic religion has in it the awareness of a mediating link between God the Absolute and the relative world. And whatever the name and form which this link takes in other religions, it is right and proper for Christians to see it as the ontological parallel of the concept of Christ and in some way as identical with or analogous to Christ. In *The Unknown Christ of Hinduism* he sees Iswara as the mediating link relating the Absolute to the world, and interprets it as being "one way or another identical with Christ". Iswara represents an inevitable universal principle present in all religions, to mediate between the One and the Manifold, the Absolute and the Relative, between Brahman and the world.

> This is, in my opinion, not just a Vedantic problem; in the ultimate analysis the Amir of the Koran, the Logos of Plotinus and the Thathagatha of Buddhism, for example, arise out of similar needs in their respective traditions to find an ontological link between these two opposed and apparently irreconcilable poles — the Absolute and the Relative.[29]

Elsewhere, Panikkar says that Christ the "Only Mediator" is present and active in all authentic religions, "whatever the forms or name". Christians give the name "Christ" to this "ever-transcending but equally ever-humanly immanent Mystery" of the Mediator; other religions may rightly give other names. And the meeting of Christianity with other religions has to take place at this level of "parallel mediating symbols".[30]

Thirdly, do the different names and forms of the Mediator in the other religions represent the same saving faith-commitment to Jesus Christ as in Christianity? Or are they contrary faiths needing conversion to Christ in some sense? Panikkar explores this question openly. He does not say that they express an identical faith. The meeting between "Christ" and his parallels in other religions should lead to the detecting of "points of convergence and discrepancy with all the required qualifications".[31] Among these required qualifications, the most important is that in any religious complex the essential faith should be distinguished from both the belief-system and the cultural pattern of life and thought in which it finds expression. In the discussion on spirituality he made a similar distinction between spirituality and the rites, structures and dogmas of a religion. But here we need some understanding of what according to Panikkar constitutes a religion.

For Panikkar, Christianity is the total complex of "Christendom, church, Christ". If Christendom is "the social-historical crystallization" and the church "the sacramental structure", Christ indicates "the transcendent mystery which nurtures the two other levels". All religions are total complexes of this kind. "If a Christian could call these three levels Christendom, Church, Christ, a Buddhist may call them Sangha, Dharma, Nirvana; a Hindu Sampradaya, Karma, Brahma; a Muslim

Umma, Qur'an, Allah." He adds that these threefold levels are true in "any human condition, not excluding the so-called Humanistic and Secular". A believer will admit the distinction between culture, religion and faith but not their separation. Panikkar does not accept the separation between *paramarthikas* and *vyvaharikas*; and this is precisely what he affirms in theandrism.[32] But there is a movement from the circumference to the centre and back to the circumference within the circle as one moves from culture through religion to faith and back. In this sense the centre of religion is faith.

At the centre, where faith is an act of trust in a transcendent mystery, it has to be expressed in a certain kind of awareness. Even at this level of awareness, one has to distinguish, without separating, between spirituality, myth and belief. "Reasoning reason is only one aspect, almost a technique, of the logos. The logos is a certain intelligibility... but it is not primarily reason. Rather it is word... it is the revelation, the very symbol of Being — the *logos* is along with the *epos*, the *mythos* and *ainos*, one of the four ingredients of consciousness."[33] Ultimately for Panikkar myth is the more intelligible language of faith; rational formulations are secondary.

Panikkar says that "belief articulates the myth which we believe without believing that we believe in it. To believe is not to hold a belief as one holds an object of knowledge; it is simply the act of believing — which may express itself in different formulations, but does not believe in them."[34]

This clarification is necessary to understand two points he makes regarding the condition for the exploration of convergence and divergence between the Christ-symbols in different religions.

1. A faith needs beliefs to express it, but no articulation of a faith in belief is an adequate expression of that faith. Therefore comparison and contrast at the level of beliefs can never be the final answer in relation to the convergence or divergence of different religions at the level of their faith-core. Panikkar says: "I am not simplistically saying that all beliefs are merely expressions of one and the same Faith. In any event the act of faith is not only transcendent uniting us with what surpasses but also transcendental. It exceeds all possible formulations."[35] Therefore, at the level of beliefs we cannot determine the extent of convergence and divergence among faiths.

2. Related to the tension between faith and belief is the question of the essential Christian faith which is to be translated from the conceptual framework of Western culture to that of Eastern cultures. For instance, is

"the space-time category" of historicity and individuality of Christ-Incarnate-in-Jesus an essential aspect of the faith in Christ, or is it to be considered culturally bound and therefore to be transcended in translation? Panikkar thinks it is culturally bound and not part of the essence of the Christian faith. "The historically trained western mind has taken spatio-temporal coordinates as the central point of reference to answering the question who Jesus is, being well aware though that this answer is not sufficient." Panikkar continues to say that in the translation of the truth of Jesus Christ "outside the Semitic world" this central point of reference cannot stand if the translation is to be more than "only a verbal one". He asks whether people of Eastern religions and cultures who are "expecting no Messiah" are to be "circumcised in their minds" and become culturally Semitic before they can accept the Christian faith. And he reminds us that the first Jerusalem council of the church decided against circumcision for gentile Christians!

Similarly Christ is Man, not a single individual man. "Christ has human nature indeed, he is Man, but he is not a person. He is divine person, the Second Person of the Trinity having assumed human nature... Christ is man, but not *one* man, a single individual; he is divine person incarnated, a divine person in hypostatic union with human nature."[36]

At this point Panikkar is asking the church to move away from the semitically formulated kerygma of the Christian faith to the "real Christ", the "naked Christ". He is pleading for "a *dekerygmatisation* of faith". "The *kerygma* has its place, as has also myth" but it cannot be "identified without qualification with the reality".[37]

Panikkar rejects the criticism that this approach is docetic. In fact, says Panikkar, he speaks of Christ as the central symbol of Reality because "more neutral symbols such as God, Spirit, Truth and the like" can become expressions of "a disincarnate principle, a nonhistorical epiphany and often an abstraction" leading to an "impersonal undiscriminated (ultimately inhuman) unity", or eventual dualism; but the emphasis on the Christ-symbol avoids this docetic danger because it "stands for that centre of reality, that crystallization point around which the human and the divine and the material can grow".[38]

Allowing for the difficulties of going behind the beliefs to the underlying faiths of religions and of translating the Christian faith into the conceptual frameworks in which other faiths have expressed themselves, Panikkar is of the opinion that "the transcendent convergence" at the level of the different mediating symbols of various religions may be much greater than generally assumed on the basis of the apparent categorical divergences. Therefore people belonging to different religions and having seemingly "conflicting interpretations" may still be pointing towards identical or "complementary" aspects of the same Transcendent Mystery. Panikkar uses the symbol of the rainbow to denote the nature of the possible harmony that may exist.

Whether this hypothesis is valid or not will be known only when the dialogue encounter among religions takes place at the level of their different Christ-symbols. Such a meeting does take place on the common ground of the Mediator principle, but not on the ground of the name which Christian faith gives to it. "Christian principles have no *a priori* paradigmatic value so that it is not a question of just searching for possible equivalents elsewhere. The fair procedure is to start from all possible starting points and witness to the actual encounter taking place along the way."[39]

Church of Jesus Christ — a sacrament

Given Trinitarian spirituality and the universal Christ as the framework of interfaith and intrafaith dialogue, what are the separate and common futures of religions? More specifically, what is the nature and function of Christianity in relation to other living religions and secular faiths?

According to Panikkar, the world today is at a particularly important stage in the evolution of humanity. If we look closely we can see that there is a movement of the Spirit in all world religions, new religions and ideological faiths, in the direction of a new unity of the sacred and the profane. World religions are "secularising"; a-religious movements are becoming "sacralised"; and new religions embracing the secular and the religious in new forms are emerging. "The progressively growing awareness and openness to the community of mankind, the world, nature and history" has led the church too in the path of renewal so as to be able to provide the leaven of the gospel to the transformation of the temporal realm of world community. But the call is for a more radical renewal. It involves moving forward, "beyond what we call Christianity, beyond, I am tempted to add, even the institutional and visible Church".[40] The signs of the times — and "the Spirit who reveals himself in them" — invite the church "to open wide the doors of oikumene, to break down the walls (of protection once upon a time, but nowadays of separation) and enter into the only true experience of Christ in human and cosmic koinonia".

Is this ecumenical ecumenism alien to the nature of the church and its faith? Panikkar thinks not. The church is "centred upon the authentic and living person of Jesus Christ" and, as such, claims that "she is the place where Christ is fully revealed". What does this mean? It certainly means that the church cannot accept itself as "one religion among others". But that need not be interpreted as affirming that "she is *the* religion for the whole mankind", the only true religion. The church's claim is that she is "the end and plenitude of every religion", "the fullest of all religions and the perfection of each religion". Therefore the church is the sign (sacrament) in the universe of religions, of the irresistible movement of the Spirit "towards the *apokatastasis*, the restoration of all in Christ". Her function is to participate in the life of all religions as "the yeast which leavens the lump and the light which drives away shadows and (to) be the victim whose immolation saves and purifies all things".[41]

Here Panikkar visualizes for the church both an identity of sacramental vocation and a spiritual immolation in other religions. It is thus that the Christian koinonia and the human-cosmic koinonia, Christian ecumenism and ecumenical ecumenism become integral to each other.

Of course the Spirit has given religions special vocations of their own in the movement towards spiritual plenitude. The church must accept the ferment of other religions and assimilate it through its Trinitarian redefinition of spirituality and Christ. At this point Panikkar warns again: "If we remain attached exclusively to the 'Saviour', to his humanity and his historicity, we block, in a manner of speaking, the coming of the Spirit and thus revert to a stage of exclusive iconolatry."[42]

In this light, relationship between various religions should be "not one of assimilation or of antagonism but of mutual fecundations".[43] This phrase "mutual fecundation" occurs repeatedly in Panikkar's writings. In fact he expects the dialogue among religious and secular faiths to result in "interpenetration, mutual fecundation and a mutation in self-interpretation" of all religious traditions. This would take place in such a way that each religion will see itself as "a dimension of the other in a *sui generis* co-inherence or co-involvement, just as each human being is potentially the whole of mankind, though each one develops and actualizes only a finite number of possibilities in a united way."[44]

Here what Panikkar has in mind is "an existential unity of dynamic character" within the diversity of religions. Not just at the mystical level but on the "concrete level of human life". It is out of a recognition of the historicity of human beings and the function of religion in the present kairos of world history that Panikkar pleads for "a dynamic historical convergence" as the goal for religions.[45] This will be made possible as a result of the organic growth of each religion from within, through mutual fecundation in the larger Christ of God.

The category of "growth" is central to Panikkar's theology of the dynamic convergence of religions. For him, in fact, the whole cosmos is developing. "There is an expansion of the whole universe. In a word, there is real growth in man, in the world, and I would also add, in God, at least inasmuch as neither immutability nor change are categories of divine. The divinity is constant newness, pure act."[46] So long as history continues, religions too must grow. This constant growth is fundamental to a sacramental theology.

> God is at work in all religions. The Christian kerygma does not proclaim a new God, but the *mirabelia* of God of which the mystery of Christ hidden in God is the alpha and omega. The very expression in fact is declaring that Christ is not yet "finished", not "discovered" until the "last moment" or the "end" has come. The process itself is still open-eneded.[47]

Panikkar adds that the process of growth means, for Christianity as well as for other religions, "continuity and development", but also "transformation and revolution". It does "not exclude mutation" and even "death and resurrection". "How Hinduism needs to grow or how Christianity or modern humanism has to grow, we may not yet know."[48]

"The being of Christianity is a becoming," says Panikkar.[49] Therefore a Neo-Christianity structured for the sacramental vocation envisaged here must grow out of the present Christianity. It involves more than simple development or explication. "In growth there is continuity as well as novelty." Panikkar indicates two lines of such a growth today.

One is the line of Christian collaboration with adherents of other faiths in common human efforts. This is set within the framework of Christ mediating God to all humanity and the whole cosmos. Panikkar affirms that "all human activities that have redemptive value offer a common ground for cooperation between Christians and non-Christians". In this cooperative work for fellow human beings and creation, the non-Christian works out "the internal grace" and the Christian witnesses to Christ and lets him "act through the Christian's presence and action for the fulfilment of redemption".[50] Panikkar is deeply conscious of the crisis of modern culture and the necessity for a theandric secular-sacred unity approach to humanize contemporary societies. "Man is weary of certain dehumanizing trends in established religions. Humanism may be a healthy reaction. Currently, modern ideologies and so-called technocracies of every sort are also seen as dehumanizing forces. Not only are a transcendental heaven and an eternal hell now viewed as dehumanizing, but society, techniques, modern cities etc. are also seen as deleterious to Man."[51] It is in this context that religious and secular humanists have to be involved in the process of the humanization of culture. Panikkar recognizes that the religious and secular faiths have different interpretations of the human predicament. But he sees the possibility of a dynamic convergence in defining the goals and new models for human liberation in the socio-cultural sphere, facilitating cooperation.

This, Panikkar illustrates through a discussion of Buddhist, Christian and Secular Humanist answers to the human predicament. What is common to them is "a double assumption: (1) man is an unachieved being; (2) this achievement is the real Man." It is possible to have a dialogue on the nature of human destiny as seen by the three answers, and to develop a model for common action in the temporal sphere. It is in the name of human liberation that "Buddhism wants to annihilate Man", "Christianity wants to divinize Man" and "Humanism wants to humanize Man".

On one thing Panikkar is clear. The traditional "one-sided solutions" will not work, as for instance the traditional idea of Christendom with its control of the state. "Christendom is the socio-religious structure of Christianity and as such is a religion like any other." Obviously Panikkar envisages a "secular" framework with equality under law for all religions.

The other line points to the building of indigenous churches within the milieu of other religions and cultures.

The church is constituted by a community of people drawn from many religions and cultures, acknowledging Jesus as the revelation of Christ; and in the sacramental theology they see the church as the sign of the plenitude towards which Christ is calling the religions and cultures in which the church sojourns. Therefore Panikkar thinks that the church should provide the model, within its fellowship, of that destiny, by assimilating and perfecting their spiritual treasures.

Panikkar's category of growth within the framework of universal Trinity and Christ involves for Christianity an approach which goes beyond the translation of established Christian truths and their communication. He calls for going beyond mere "utilization" or "interpretation" of other cultures and religions to promote already formulated Christian beliefs and structures. It requires opening the church to new truths and going out of the house already built to put up tents outside in "the crossroads outside the walls" — for the time being. For the history of Christianity shows that "precisely where the Christian message succeeded in transforming a society it was never by such utilization, but on the contrary by its being assimilated — the Christian word is incarnated — by that particular religion and culture: the Christian fact being the leaven."[52]

In fact Paul and John and the church fathers may be seen as involved in a double process of "utilizing" and "being utilized". It was through this process that the truths of Christ were defined and new developments beyond established definitions took place through the incorporation of "the fuller meaning of pre-Christian ideas seen in the sight of Christ".

> No Christian doctrine of the Trinity nor any Christology existed before its expression in Gentile and Jewish categories... The first Christians did not "utilize" Greek or other thought-categories of the times in order to convey what had not yet found expression. On the contrary only by means of these categories — Jewish and Gentile — could the Christian experience be expressed and understood at all... They were not utilizing Greek concepts to express one single Christian institution, but they had a different understanding of the Christian fact, perhaps because they were carried away by the very concepts they used. One could almost say that they were utilized, used by those very concepts.[53]

If it is argued that the situation is different today when the church has an established definition, Panikkar would reply, first, that much of the established tradition "seems to be exhausted, . . . effete, when it tries to express the Christian message in a meaningful way for our times",[54] and second, Christianity (as well as other religions) has grown in the past only by the stimulus of incorporating ideas once considered foreign or denounced as heretical, and it cannot be different in the new situation. But such incorporation is to be achieved not just by transplantation but by reinterpretation.

It is in this context that Panikkar maintains that Western Christianity as it now exists is "the ancient paganism, or to be more precise the complex Hebrew-Hellenic-Graeco-Latin-Celtic-Gothic-Modern religion converted to Christ more or less successfully"; and that therefore "Indian Christianity should be Hinduism itself converted — or Islam, Buddhist, whatever it may be".[55]

NOTES

[1] *New Catholic Encycolpedia*, New York, London, McGraw Hill, 1967, Vol. 2, p.724.
[2] *Documents of Vatican II*. References in the preceding section and from the "Dogmatic Constitution of the Church", paras 1, 13-17. "Pastoral Constitution on the Church in the Modern World", paras 19-22. "Decree on the Missionary Activity of the Church", para. 3. "Declaration on the Relation of the Church to Non-Christian Religions", para. 2.

[3] *Theological Investigations*, Vol. V, 1966.
[4] Translated by W.Y. Dyck, New York, Seabury, 1978, pp.311-321.
[5] *Ibid.*, p.316.
[6] *Ibid.*, pp.318-321.
[7] London, Burns & Oates, 1963.
[8] *Ibid.*, pp.74-75.
[9] *Ibid.*, p.105.
[10] J. Neuner ed., *Christian Revelation and World Religions*, London, Burns & Oates, 1967, p.10.
[11] *Service and Salvation*, Nagpur Theological Conference on Evangelisation, ed. Joseph Pathrapankal, CMI, Bangalore, Theological Publications in India, 1973.
[12] "Are Non-christian Religions Salvific?", *ibid.*, p.197.
[13] *Ibid.*, pp.197-198.
[14] "The Salvific Value of Non-Christian Religions", *ibid.*, pp.229-230.
[15] W. Buhlmann, *The Search for God*, Maryknoll, NY, Orbis, 1980, pp.167f.
[16] *Ibid.*, pp.41-42.
[17] *Ibid.*, p.169.
[18] London, Darton, Longman & Todd.
[19] *Trinity and World Religions*, Bangalore, CISRS, 1970, p.43.
[20] *Cross Currents*, 1983, p.148.
[21] Bangalore, CISRS, 1968.
[22] *Pilgrims of the Way*, preface by Murray Rogers, Bangalore, CISRS, 1966. Part of it was published in *The Ecumenical Review*, Vol. 38, No. 1, 1986.
[23] *Cross Currents, op. cit.*, p.147.
[24] *Trinity and World Religions, op. cit.*, p.72.
[25] *Ibid.*, p.80.
[26] *The Unknown Christ of Hinduism, op. cit.*, p.67.
[27] *Ibid.*, p.14; "The Meaning of Christ's Name in the Universal Economy of Salvation", *Service and Salvation, op. cit.*, p.242.
[28] *Trinity and World Religions, op. cit.*, p.52.
[29] *Ibid.*, p.148.
[30] *The Intra-religious Dialogue*, New York, Paulist Press, 1978, pp.36-37.
[31] *Ibid.*, pp.36-37.
[32] *Cross Currents*, pp.190-191.
[33] *Ibid.*, p.214.
[34] *Myth, Faith and Hermeneutics*, New York, Paulist Press, 1979, p.5.
[35] *Ibid.*, pp.20-21.
[36] "The Meaning of Christ's Name", *Service and Salvation, op. cit.*, pp.242-248.
[37] "Category of Growth in Contemporary Religion", *Harvard Theological Review*, 1973, p.115.
[38] *The Unknown Christ, op. cit.*, p.27.
[39] *Ibid.*, p.37.
[40] *Trinity and World Religions, op. cit.*, p.55.
[41] *Ibid.*, pp.55-56.
[42] *Ibid.*, p.56.
[43] *The Unknown Christ, op. cit.*, p.12.
[44] *Ibid.*, p.95.
[45] Dankried Reetz, "Raymond Panikkar's Theology of Religion", *Religion and Society*, 1968, No. 3.
[46] *Harvard Theological Review, op. cit.*, p.135.
[47] *The Unknown Christ, op. cit.*, p.168.
[48] *Intra-religious Dialogue, op. cit.*, p.72.
[49] Reetz, *op. cit.*, p.41.

[50] "Common Grounds for Christian-non Christian Collaboration", *Religion and Society*, 1958, p.31.
[51] *Intra-religious Dialogue, op. cit.*, pp.86-87.
[52] *Ibid.*, p.58.
[53] *Ibid.*, p.59.
[54] *Ibid.*, p.61.
[55] *Christian Revelation and World Religions, op. cit.*, p.169.

3. Common Quest for a New Humanism: Towards Dialogical Participation

A. DEVELOPMENTS IN PROTESTANT MISSIONARY ECUMENICAL THOUGHT

1. Partnership against secularism — Jerusalem 1928

The meetings of the International Missionary Council, first in Jerusalem 1928 and then in Tambaram 1938, dealt at length with the Christian approach to other religions and secularism. They played a major role in the evolution of the main trends in the theology of religions within Protestant missionary circles, and eventually in the modern ecumenical movement as expressed in the World Council of Churches.

The "absoluteness of Christianity" was always the basic presupposition of Western Christian missions. How then was Christian mission to define its attitude to non-Christian religions?

The early missionaries thought of other religions as "heathenish idolatries" and as works of the devil. The Science of Religion developed as a discipline during the latter half of the nineteenth century and the first decades of the twentieth. As a result Max Muller's evolutionary theory, which saw the history of the world in its religious aspect as a development towards Christianity and non-Christian religions as preliminary stages in that process, became more and more popular. From this arose the missionary theology of T.S. Slater and J.N. Farquhar in India. It saw Christianity as the "fulfilment" and "crown" of all other religions, the ultimate answer to the "seeking" which other religions represented.

By Jerusalem 1928 it was clear that the gathering force of political nationalism among non-Western peoples involved not only a resurgence of traditional religions but also, side by side with it, the dominant influence upon them of Western secular culture and anti-religious secularism. J.H. Oldham was eager to build up a missionary approach in which the significance of the "human values" of secular culture and the "spiritual values" of ancient religions were transcended and fulfilled in the absoluteness of Christianity. A section in the Jerusalem missionary conference was planned with this aim.

Rufus Jones, in his presentation at the Jerusalem meeting, sought precisely to evolve such a theology of encounter with secularism and other religions. Jones spoke on the one hand of the need for Christian missions to look upon non-Christian religions as "allies" in their encounter against secularism and their endeavour to preserve spiritual values; and on the other of Christian missions as being engaged in the task of fulfilling the human values of secularism against traditional religious culture.

In the discussion W.E. Hocking regarded secularism as "the decisive missionary problem" and wanted Christian missions to cooperate with other religions in building the religious foundation for the "coming world civilization".

Hendrik Kraemer and others from the European continent were critical of considering the central mission of Christianity in terms of its contribution to "values", religious or secular, because the approach was anthropocentric and denied the transcendant character of the revelation in Christ.

The Jerusalem report was a compromise. It recognized several values of non-Christian religions as well as of secular civilization "as part of the truth":

> that sense of the majesty of God and the consequent reverence in worship which are conspicuous in Islam; the deep sympathy of the world's sorrow and unselfish search for the way of escape which are at the heart of Buddhism; the desire for contact with ultimate reality conceived as spiritual which is prominent in Hinduism; the belief in a moral order of the universe and consequent insistence on moral conduct which is inculcated by Confucianism; the disinterested pursuit of truth and human welfare which are often found in those who stand for secular civilization but do not accept Christ as their Lord and Saviour.

It spoke of the need of secular values to be dedicated to Christ if they are "not to be debased into self-assertive exploitation and service of greed". It called on the non-Christian religions to "hold fast to faith in the unseen and eternal in face of the growing materialism of the world; to cooperate with us against the evils of secularism", to "join with us in the study of Jesus Christ", and to "share with us the pardon and life that we have found in Christ".[1]

The American Commission report, *Rethinking Missions: a Laymen's Enquiry After One Hundred Years*,[2] was the work of Hocking and Jones and it expressed the position they had advocated at the Missionary Council meeting. As a philosopher-theologian, Hocking elaborated the approach. His lectures on "Living Religions and a World Faith" are important in this respect, as are his many other writings. A brief survey of his position is appropriate here.

W.E. Hocking

Hocking defines religion as "passion for righteousness conceived as a cosmic demand".[3] In any civilization, religion provides the "cosmic" spiritual support to the "moral" pattern of life and relations and a constant ferment directing people to a destiny beyond the earthly city. The question today is how the world civilization now coming into being can build an enduring relation between the moral and mystic dimensions. The world community needs a "world faith".

Among traditional religions now existing in the world, there is a basic unity in regard to the essence of religion, but in their expressions in "creed, code and ritual", developed in isolation from each other, the religions are not only plural but also diverse and even conflicting at many points. Especially the ritual side, though the "least significant", is the "most enduring" in every religion, because it is "the vehicle of feeling"; and at this level, all religions tend to emphasize their distinctiveness. A world faith cannot emerge either through an aggressive religion claiming to be "the only way", the absolute religion, or through the effort at producing a "synthesis" of the different religions. A world faith can emerge in our situation only by each religion undertaking a "reconception" of itself from within in the light of other religions, within the context of a partnership in the mission of fighting irreligion and pursuing a common search for truth.

In this process, mutuality between religions is basic. But every religion grows both in self-understanding and in its capacity to interpret and assimilate the truths of other religions. "In proportion as any religion grows in self-understanding through grasping its own essence, it grasps the essence of all religion and gains in power to interpret its various forces."[4] It leads to each particular religion becoming universalized by relating its particularity to the universality of faith.

Hocking sees a very significant role for Christianity and its central symbol of Jesus Christ.

In the present historical situation, Hocking says: "No religion can become a religion for Asia which does not fuse the spiritual genius of Asia with that of Western Christianity; and not alone the genius of Asia but that of each of its major great religions." Western Christianity is important because of its historical relation with Western culture and the forces produced within that culture are now moulding the modern world civilization; it gives Christianity a unique understanding of the religious problems of modernity. But the missionary idea of radically displacing Asian religions by Western Christianity is both wrong and impossible.

Western Christianity has to become Asian along two paths — one, by assimilating the spiritual truths of Asian religions and reconceiving itself, and two, by Western Christianity becoming incarnate within Asian religions through a reconception taking place within them.

Hocking believes that empirically Christianity is "not yet ready to serve as a world religion". But it has the potentiality to reconceive itself and to assimilate the truths of other religions and become truly universal; it is "on the way to become universal". Its Christ-symbol and its unique awareness of the "religious problems of the emerging civilization" give it a certain leadership among religions. But that leadership can be actualized only if it is ready to "acknowledge its own continuing need for reconception, in view of its present unfinishedness and also of the depth and breadth of the religious experience of other lands".[5] Presented not as the "only way" but as the disclosures of the "truth" of all ways, which all religions can intrinsically discern, the Christ-symbol has universal appeal. "As a privilege, the Christ-symbol 'will draw all men', as a threat never."[6]

Hocking rejects the idea of revelation unrelated to the history of the search for religious truths. "The idea of a divine plan considered as a dated product of God's wisdom and goodness wholly unimaginable to man is, I fear, an ingenious invention of St Paul."[7] Hocking discerns a universal revelation of God and a universal faith-response as present in some measure in all religions; and Jesus Christ is "the making-fully-explicit of the universal faith".[8] The religious insights into "victory over suffering and death" and into "divine forgiveness" made explicit by Christ are universal. In Jesus "the general symbol of mediator, the Christ, becomes a literal particular".[9]

Here Hocking specifically refers to Karl Barth's criticism of the Jerusalem 1928 approach, and challenges Barth's views on revelation and mission.

> The missionary (Barth says) is servant not of man but the Word of God. The divine Grace is to be announced as a miracle, not as a bridge that one may build, not as a sublimation of the natural. Hence the missionary is not to fraternize nor accept the fellowship of fallen faiths.[10]

It is in the theology of revelation that there is fundamental conflict between Hocking and Barth. After the thirties the theology of missions on the whole moved away from Hocking to Barth.

2. Revelation against religion — Tambaram 1938

Let us look at some of the critical questions raised especially by European theologians, with regard to the approach which the Jerusalem conference had taken.

Karl Barth, writing in the *Student World* on "Questions which 'Christianity' must face", [11] challenged both Jerusalem's reading of the historical crisis and its theological viewpoint. According to him the chief aspect of the situation that obtained in the Western world in the third decade of the twentieth century was not the expansion of the eighteenth and nineteenth century liberal philosophies, but the emergence of "absolutely new religions" like Communism, Fascism and "Americanism" (God of health and comfort), in all of which "the age-old natural religion" was at work. And in the non-Western world there was resurgence of ancient religions. Therefore it was to the "religious" humanity, not to the "secular" humanity, that the gospel must address itself.

Secondly, Barth criticized Jerusalem for "bothering their heads for a whole week, not so much about what the Gospel means as about the 'values' of the non-Christian religions". Such bridge-building as Jerusalem represented was "howling with the wolves" and must be abandoned without reserve in favour of "the missionary campaign which tells men what God has revealed and what therefore they are obliged to hear, for God has revealed it".The great temptation which Christianity faces today, said Barth, is that of "overlooking essentials"; it is the temptation to compromise with one or another of these religions, thereby avoiding the "offence" inherent in the gospel. "In the midst of the confusion and difficulty of our times, the Christian message ought to be proclaimed in all its purity, not confused with the voices of other religions." Christianity should understand itself as the church, that is, "the one place where man listens and God speaks in the midst of a world of loquacious and brilliant religions". It is not the task of Christian mission to cater to human needs as other religions understand them or other "gods" can satisfy, but to perceive the common need and the common question of which they are unaware and of which it can "speak to them with authority" because the Christian is in solidarity with all human beings in a common wretchedness.

Barth elsewhere spoke of proclaiming Divine Grace as a miracle, "not as a sublimation of nature". In contrast, Jerusalem 1928 appeared to him as a variation upon "the ancient and seductive melody of the Serpent. Grace does not destroy nature, it perfects it."[12]

The protest against the anthropocentricity of religions in the name of the theo-centricity of Revelation is characteristic of the Dialectical Theology of Karl Barth, Emil Brunner, Visser 't Hooft and others. Under their leadership, it made a tremendous impact on the church's struggle against the "new pagan religions" like Nazism in the West. It was through Hendrik Kraemer that the missionary theology of world religions in the world missionary movement changed in the same direction. It may be useful, therefore, to look more closely at Karl Barth's own interpretation of the relation between Christ and religion.

Karl Barth: revelation as abolition of religion

In his commentary on the Epistle to the Romans, especially dealing with Romans 7, Karl Barth, in the light of the cross of Christ, equates Religion with Law, which manifests the maturity of sin as it works death, and points out that Divine Grace in Christ puts an end to the religion-law-death vicious circle. Though Barth is dealing here with the religions of Israel and Christianity, what he says may be seen as applying to religion in general.

Since humanity everywhere retains "the memory of the lost direct relationship with God", none can escape religion. It represents the attempts of the godless person to be reconciled with God on his/her own terms, attempts which alienate him/her all the more from God. Religion in all its forms can be "defined by the all-embracing word — sin". "The possibility of religion enables the essentially godless man to attain the full maturity of his godlessness by bringing forth a rich and most conspicuous harvest of fruit unto death."[13] "Religion compels us to the perception that God is not to be found in religion. Religion makes us know that we are competent to advance no single step. Religion is the final human possibility, commanding us to halt." In fact "death is the meaning of religion"; "religion is abyss; it is terror. There demons appear... Religion is that human necessity in which the power exercised over men by sin is clearly demonstrated."[14]

This does not mean that religion is all evil and completely without value. Far from it. Comparative religion can rightly speak of an evolutionary development in the history of human religion from the lowest to the highest forms of it; and it "reaches its highest and purest peak in the Law of Israel" and Israel's prophetic tradition. It is indeed possible to distinguish between good and evil, between good, better and best religion, indeed to speak of religion "as the last step in human progress". But the whole of it, the totality, both its good and bad, is exposed by the cross of Christ as human self in rebellion against God. For we should not forget the fact that it was the religious best, church, not the world, which crucified Christ.

Nor is there any escape from religion through materialism or mysticism. Materialism may be "a more plausible interpretation of the general course of the history of humanity" than idealism. But it is no answer to the crisis of religion. At best it exposes only the godlessness of religion. And "the mystic's way of denial is a blind alley", revealing the futility of religion. "Religion as the final human possibility commands us to halt. Religion brings us to the place where we must wait, in order that God may confront us — on the other side of the frontier of religion." "All human religion is directed towards an end beyond itself, and the end is Christ."

Thus Divine Grace in Christ cannot be considered a part of human religion, of any religion. Nor is it a new religion. "Golgotha is the end of the law and the frontier of religion." Jesus Christ is "the New Man standing beyond all piety". Christ leads to "a fearless relativity of all religions" and brings them to their end. Christ is the end even of the Christian religion. "There is no sinless Christian. If thou chancest upon such a man, he is no Christian, but an anti-Christ." "Rightly understood there are no Christians; there is only the eternal opportunity of becoming Christian — an opportunity at once accessible and inaccessible to all men." "It is obvious that the opposition between the Church and the Gospel is final and all-embracing. The Gospel dissolves the Church and the Church dissolves the Gospel."[15] The Grace which reconciles men and women to God is "unattainable by men except in the miracle of the Absolute Moment" of divine self-revelation in grace; it is "the unexpected new Divine occurrence among them". Does this occur "within the church or outside it"? "That question is trivial," says Barth. The miracle of the Absolute Moment has no continuity as religious history. Christ touches human history as "the tangent touches the circle, that is without touching it".

In *Church Dogmatics* Karl Barth attempts a theological interpretation of religion. The English translation of the section has the title: "Revelation of God as the Abolition of Religion".[16]

The essay begins by affirming two truths about human beings: that the human person is "the subject of religion"; and that whether he or she knows it or not, the human person is the object of the revelation of God's word in Jesus Christ. Since the latter has primacy, theology seeks to know "the nature of religion from the standpoint of God's revelation" rather than revelation in the light of "immanent definitions of the nature of religion". For revelation, distinctions between religions, whether between higher and lower, good and bad, traditional, reformed and modern or any other, has no significance. Evolutionary, relativist and sceptical interpretations of the history of religions, or even the mystic and atheistic self-criticism of religion, are irrelevant. They all belong to the "magic circle of religion". The important thing is to understand the human situation which religion represents — "understand it even in the dark and terrifying perplexity of it — not because it can see any meaning in the situation as such, but because it acquires a meaning from outside, from Jesus Christ".

Barth's theology of religion includes the following theses:

First, "religion is unbelief" — it is "the one great concern of godless man". From the standpoint of God's revelation of himself in Christ as God and Lord, human religion as such is "resistance to it". It is the human effort to replace the divine reality by "a concept of God arbitrarily and wilfully evolved by man". It is "unbelief, idolatry, self-righteousness".

> If a man tries to grasp at the truth of himself he tries to grasp at it *a priori* — in religion he ventures to grasp at God. Because it is a grasping, religion is the contradiction of revelation, the concentrated attitude and activity which is directly opposed to faith... We cannot therefore interpret the attempt as a harmonious cooperating of man with the revelation of God, as though religion were a kind of outstretched hand which is filled by God in his revelation...

In Romans 1, Acts 14 and 17, it is not "profane and secular attitude" but worship offered by the human being in loyalty to what he regards as divine that is "roundly denied by God's revelation in Christ"; that is, "the worship of things which by nature are not gods at all". In the light of the self-revelation of the truth, "our human being and activity is seen to be in its ultimate and profound reality a fight against the truth". It is only because God is the creator that "we can commit the sin of idolatry" which is the human struggle "to storm heaven". Therefore revelation has no "link-up with a human religion which is already present and practised"; it "displaces it, just as religion previously displaced revelation".

> Jesus Christ does not fill out and improve all the different attempts of man to think of God and to represent him according to his own standard... he replaces and completely outbids those attempts, putting them in the shadows to which they belong... The revelation of God in Jesus Christ maintains that our justification and sanctification, our conversion and our salvation, have been brought about and achieved once for all in Jesus Christ.

Secondly, Karl Barth strongly stresses that, because religion is unbelief, Christian theology cannot distinguish between Christian and non-Christian religions. In fact, Barth maintains that "it is our business as Christians to apply this judgment first and most acutely to ourselves; and to others, the non-Christians, only in so far as we recognize ourselves in them". Concretely this judgment of religion as unbelief should embrace "our Christian conception of God and the things of God, our Christian theology, our Christian worship, our forms of Christian fellowship and order, our Christian morals, poetry and art, our attempts to give individual and social form to the Christian life, our Christian strategy and tactics in the interest of our Christian cause, in short our Christianity". Barth points out that throughout biblical history, revelation had to oppose the religion of revelation. Indeed, "by trying to resist and conquer other religions, we put ourselves on the same level. They too appeal to this or that immanent truth in them." In fact, it is Barth's assertion that the history of Christianity as religion even in the future will always remain in the realm of unbelief.

If this is the interpretation of religion in the light of the self-revelation of God in Jesus Christ, what is the locus of the revelation in human history? Where is the revelation in Christ given to humanity? Barth says that the church of Christ is that locus. Not because it is better or higher than other religions as religion, but because it stands open to the judgment of revelation, confessing itself as sinful. That is to say, the church can be spoken of as "true religion" in the sense and "only in the sense, in which we speak of a 'justified sinner'".

Thus "where it shows all religion to be false, it can also create true religion". Revelation negates religion as unbelief but it can also justify and sanctify it.

> Religion can just as well be exalted in revelation, even though the judgment still stands. It can be upheld by it and concealed in it. It can be justified by it, and — we must at once add — sanctified. Revelation can adopt religion and mark it off as true religion.

Not only it can. It does. And therefore we need have no hesitation in saying that the Christian religion is the true religion. It is so "as an event of the grace of God in Jesus Christ", "an act of divine creation", and "election" in Jesus Christ. It is only through divine forgiveness in Jesus Christ that the Christian religion becomes true.

Barth's parable of day and night illumines his theology of religion. Why is one part of the earth in day and another in night, when the earth is the same in both places? Apart from the sun, it would be night everywhere. "The fact that it is partly in the day does not derive in any sense from the nature of the particular part as such. Now it is in exactly the same way that the light of the righteousness and judgment of God falls upon the world of man's religion, upon one part of that world, upon the Christian religion, so that that religion is not in the night but in the day, it is not perverted but straight, it is not false religion, but true."

Barth goes on to point out that this election of the church in grace as the true religion among religions is not aimed to vindicate "one part of humanity as opposed to other parts of humanity". But it is rather the vindication of God "on behalf of all men and all humanity". And for this reason, the church of Christ "alone has the commission and the authority to be a missionary religion, i.e. to confront the world of religions as the one true religion with absolute self-confidence to invite and challenge it to abandon its ways and to start on the Christian way".

> The Christian religion is the sacramental area created by the Holy Spirit in which the God whose word became flesh continues to speak through the sign of His revelation.

John Carman points out that the German word which Barth uses and is translated "abolition" in the title of the chapter dealing with the theology of religion is a word used by Hegel too. It could be translated as "pickled". That is, what Barth meant was that "religion is a human reality that God destroys, preserves and takes up to a higher level". He adds: "To be sure, in the way in which Barth develops this dialectic", while all religions are judged as enmity to God, only Christianity is converted by Grace to the higher level to be the instrument of salvation.[17]

Hendrik Kraemer: biblical realism

The International Missionary Council invited Hendrik Kraemer to write the study book for its meeting in Tambaram, 1938. That was how *Christian Message in a Non-Christian World* came to be written. Through the Tambaram missionary conference and the post-Tambaram missionary theological discussions, the Barthianism of Kraemer made its impact in the world missionary movement and in the churches of Asia and Africa planted by the missions.

Barth, Brunner and Kraemer emphasize the biblical understanding of reality. It is the understanding that God is wholly other than humanity which is both creature and sinner; and that God's self-revelation in Jesus Christ by its very nature cannot "correspond to the concept of natural man", and must remain inaccessible to human beings "even when it is revealed", thus causing "offence". Kraemer uses the phrase "biblical realism" to indicate that according to the Bible reality is theocentric. It means that God is "the all-pervading centre in total reality" which is opposed to all anthropocentric endeavours "to reduce reality to a body of truths and ideals about the personality of God, the infinite value of man, the source of ethical inspiration". Here Kraemer is in complete agreement with Barth. So, says Kraemer, Jerusalem 1928 discussed the values of non-Christian religions "in a too-isolated way" on the assumption that "reason and history" were "sources" of God's self-revelation, and that the "values" were identical with "Truth". This made man the standard reference. It ends in "a vicious circle". "Christian revelation places itself against the many efforts to apprehend the totality of existence" which constitute human religion. This is the same language as that of Barth.

Nevertheless, Kraemer's approach has certain special characteristics, because of his interest both in the phenomenological study of the religious consciousness of humanity as expressed in world religions and in working out a Christian theological interpretation of that consciousness which will expose the diverse religions as expressions of the dialectic between God and human beings. He is convinced that in this dialectic human beings say "no" to the primordial divine revelation and are under constant judgment. While Barth refuses to discuss where and how God is wrestling with human beings in their religions, Kraemer thinks it justified to do so. Barth is opposed to any "natural theology" which seeks to discern God's immanent working in sinful human nature. At this point Kraemer joins Emil Brunner in his criticisms of Barth, especially the earlier Barth.

Kraemer admits that Barth "rightly asserts the dis-continuity of nature and grace, or reason with revelation, by rejecting natural theology. He will not and cannot deny *that* God works and has worked in man outside the Biblical sphere of revelation but *how* this happens he refuses to discuss." He recognizes the "legitimacy of Brunner's protest and of his combat in favour of a critical and right kind of natural theology".

A natural theology of that kind should "learn to talk in a new way about the realm of fallen creation" including human religions, so as to clarify the "*sui generis* character of the Word made flesh". It will not be an attempt to see religions either as preparation for the gospel or as pre-Christian revelation which is fulfilled in Christ.

> The function of natural theology will henceforth be, not to construe preparatory stages and draw unbroken continuous lines of religious development ending and reaching their summit in Christ, but in the light of the Christian revelation to lay bare the dialectical condition not only of the non-Christian religions but of all the human attempts towards apprehension of the totality of existence. Or to put it differently, to uncover in the light of the revelation in Christ, the different modes of God- Self- and World-consciousness of man in his religious life.[18]

For the truth is that the religious and moral achievements of human beings have in them the marks of "God's wrestling" with them. Of course, to that, the original human response to God is one of "revolt"; and religions become human efforts at self-salvation. And in this contradiction, the universal religious consciousness everywhere creates the noblest values and produces the most degrading filth. Nevertheless, "the quest of God" is the "perennially disturbing condition" of religious consciousness that biblical realism calls "sin, guilt, lostness, past recovery except by God Himself".[19] And Brunner is right, says Kraemer, in maintaining that the theological explication of this dialectic in the quest of God in religion is a function of natural theology; and that it may become a point of contact or, more realistically speaking, a point of departure between human religiosity and the gospel.

Kraemer does not hesitate to criticize Barth as not being sufficiently dialectical. In his later book *Religion and the Christian Faith*,[20] he says that Barth's thesis that religion is unbelief, although true within due limits and applicability, leaves no room for the deeper question as to whether the whole business of religion has anything to do with God, or God has anything to do with it.

Both *Religion and the Christian Faith* and the shorter book *Why Christianity of all Religions?*[21] explain Kraemer's theology of religions further. In all his works, his biblical realist analysis of the various world religions maintains the following elements.

1. Every religion is a totality, "one whole body of religious life and expression of which all the component parts are inseparably inter-related to each other and animated by the same apprehension of the totality of existence peculiar to it".[22] The peculiar apprehension of reality in every religion has not merely mental or cultural roots, but

arises from a spiritual "choice and decision" against God's sovereignty, the revelation of which is among the formative factors of all religions, whether "prophetic religions of revelation" or "naturalistic religions of trans-empirical realization". Therefore the ideas, values, and principles of a religion should be interpreted in terms of the central apprehension of that religion and not evaluated in isolation or in some other context.

2. In its historical development and reality, empirical Christianity like every other religion has been and still is "a mixture of sublimity and perversion" reflecting "the equivocal and inwardly divided state of human nature". Nevertheless there is one factor which makes Christianity different and unique, namely its openness to the judgment of the revelation of Jesus Christ.

> The truly remarkable thing about Christianity as a historical and empirical reality which differentiates it from other religions is that radical self-criticism is one of its chief characteristics because the revelation in Christ to which it testifies erects the absolute superiority of God's holy will and judgment over all life, historical Christianity included.[23]

Answering the question whether Christianity is an Absolute, Kraemer says that Christianity is the "best" religion, not only because it stands under the judging and redeeming word of God in Jesus Christ but also because it originates in and bears witness to that word revealed in Jesus Christ.

— Christianity as one of the religions is to be distinguished from the other religions, that is, for this cardinal reason: that although it enjoys its full share of human frailty, Christianity does arise out of the revelation of God in the person of Jesus Christ.[24]

— The Christian church with all her crying sins continues to exist and to be the "best" religion not because everything about it is so very good, but because it is there that the gospel is to be heard.[25]

Here the theology affirming the radical discontinuity between the Revelation and all religions including Christianity changes, through faith-response to Jesus Christ, into an affirmation of the radical discontinuity between Christianity and other religions.

3. Transcendence against transcendentalism — Tambaram 1938 and after

The crucial issue in all debates on the Barth-Brunner-Kraemer Dialectical Theology is the nature of the relation between Revelation and the process of human history. God's grace and God's kingdom — do they have any continuity with the historical traditions in which they occur as historical events? Do they become empirical historical reality in the continuum of world history whether religious or secular, transforming and directing it towards a future? Or are they so transcendentalist as only to touch the world history at certain moments and hover over it in an ever-present crisis of judgment?

In a study of Karl Barth's doctrine of revelation, Regin Prenter points out that actualism, analogism and universalism are three of its characteristics. Actualism means that "God is in the world of man only in each specific act of his self-revelation... there is no room for a being of the revealed or the revealed in the world... It has as such no extension in time, but occurs afresh each time." It has no "history as such" because every impression of revelation, every "materialization and humanization of the divine" in the sinful world is an abandonment of God as God. Since there can be no actualization of God's self-revelation in time, "there can be only analogies, likenesses, signs and images in those movements of time surrounding the moment of revelation". Here lies the capacity of human life in Jesus Christ to be "a parable of something higher despite its negativity". Through Jesus Christ, we also know that "in all times and places there has been forgiveness of sins... the miraculous outpouring on man of the abundance of God's mercy". In the eternal election of the man Jesus Christ and of all humanity in him, the universality of redemption is the certainty of God.

Barth grants that God's revelation enters the sphere of time in the word made flesh, "but it does not itself become temporal, it rather arrests the temporal before the eternal". For God's revelation as a pure act "does not lodge in the temporal, the human is not made divine, it remains human, mortal, sinful, condemned".[26]

It is this transcendentalism of divine revelation in dialectical theology, unable to become lodged in the temporal in temporal form to renew it, that has been criticized from various angles. Here we take two types of such criticism levelled against Kraemer in Tambaram 1938, represented by reviews by A.G. Hogg and P. Chenchiah of Kraemer's *Christian Message in a Non-Christian World*.

Revelation of God as Heavenly Father: A.G. Hogg

O.V. Jathana, in a doctoral thesis on "The Decisiveness of the Christ-event and the Universality of Christianity in a World of Religious Plurality"[27] has this to say on Hogg's theology of history:

> The following elements are basic to Hogg's understanding of history. (1) History is a development and God's creation grows from less to more. And there is a "purposeful evolution" in the process of history. (2) In the process of history, an issue of supreme interest alike to God and to mankind is at stake. The work of Christ is thus figured as a cosmic crisis. (3) The purpose of the universe is the evolution of a morally perfect humanity. The inner meaning of history in the temporal process unfolds itself as evolving the moral consciousness of men. (4) With Jesus the new aeon, the new age of the Spirit has begun. (5) This new age has been delayed because of the lack of human readiness and positive response and not because of God's fiats. (6) History is an integrated orderly whole in which the future is bound up with the present and the past, and the whole of humanity in a unity. (7) Teleology which is lacking in Hinduism is vital to the historical understanding of Christianity. History is an adventure of faith and not a rigidly determined process.

Jathana sums up Hogg's understanding of history as "the experience of and faith in God's absorbed activity in history", on the basis of Hogg's writings like *Karma and Redemption, Christ's Message of the Kingdom, Redemption from this World*, and *Christian Message to the Hindu.*[28]

This is the basic framework within which Hogg sees the relation between Christianity and other religions and criticizes both Farquhar's thesis that Christianity is the "crown of Hinduism" and Kraemer's theory of total discontinuity between the two.

Jesus is the self-revelation of God, that is to say, the reality of the Divine Person as "absorbed activity in history", as Jathana puts it. As the climax of the history of the self-revelation of God, Jesus Christ brings a new divine-human reality into being in the historical process. And for Hogg, it is both discontinuous and continuous with the divine self-revelation-cum-human faith-response which is the religious history of humankind.

Hogg was critical of Farquhar's thesis that Christianity is the direct fulfilment of the spiritual longings of traditional Hinduism. According to Hogg, in Hinduism there is not only a seeking but also a finding. Christianity challenges that longing-fulfilment or seeking-finding complex of Hinduism and reorients it to new longings and search before fulfilling them. "What Christ directly fulfils is not Hinduism but the need of which India has begun to be conscious, the need by making her conscious of which, He has made her no longer Hindu."[29]

Note in the passage the reference to India, that is, the Indian people. Hinduism, their religion, has expressed their deepest spiritual longings and also satisfied them in large part. What Christ has brought to the Indian people is a change in the character of these longings or felt-needs; and it is a change which moves them away from Hinduism in the traditional sense. It is the new moral and spiritual needs, which Christ himself through Christian religion and culture has awakened, that Christ is fulfilling. Thus the new longings and needs are discontinuous with their Hindu past. So is the fulfilment by Christ. On the other hand, Hinduism itself has absorbed the new consciousness and connected it with the Hindu past by selecting certain traditions from the past which are relevant to Christ, and by reformulating them. That is to say, though the patterns of conscious life and thought in Hinduism are discontinuous with Christianity, there is a spiritual centre at the heart of Hinduism which, when awakened, is continuous in some measure with the Christian faith and religion.

"Christian Attitude to Non-Christian Faith" was the title of the paper Hogg wrote for Tambaram.[30] The singular non-Christian faith is here distinguished from the plural non-Christian faiths. The plural denotes for him "those complexes of spiritual, ethical, intellectual and social elements" which we call the non-Christian religions. But the singular faith denotes, in Kraemer's words, "the religious life as present in the non-Christian religions". Is this distinction valid? This is the first question which Hogg discusses.

Just as the religious life in the Christian religion is a life "hid with Christ in God", can we discern in the non-Christian religions "a life, which although without Christ, is yet somehow a life hid in God"? Is there any such thing as a religious faith which in quality or texture is "definitely not Christian" but in which we may recognize "a two-sided communion between God and man"? Is there in such a life of faith not merely a seeking but also a finding "by contrast with which a Christian may be helped to make fresh discoveries in his own finding of God in Christ"?

Hogg is convinced that the answer to these questions is in the affirmative. Kraemer's general attitude to non-Christian faiths as expressed in his book tends "to exclude the possibility of anything really deserving the name of non-Christian faith by suggesting that these religions are a purely human phenomenon", and in no sense "an experience of Divine self-disclosure", says Hogg. He notes Kraemer's distinction between "empirical Christianity" and the Christian faith and asks whether there is not a similar distinction between empirical non-Christian religions and their faith. While Kraemer talks of God's wrestling with human beings in all religions, it is more often interpreted in Barthian terms to signify human seeking. Hogg denies the "adequacy of a purely humanistic conception of non-Christian faiths". He believes that the universal religious consciousness is the "universal manifestation of a human response (for the most part a deplorably crude, wayward and reluctant response) to God's continually active endeavour to reveal Himself to man"; and in that sense every religion is "founded on what is, in some sense, revelation", a divine effort of disclosure.

If this is true, then it is necessary to distinguish between "the content of the revelation" on which a religion is founded and "the ideas and concepts" derived from the apprehension of the revelation. Here there is the inevitable "intrusion of a fallible human element into the revelation as apprehended and witnessed to". This is true of biblical religion and must be even more true of other religions. Therefore, in interpreting religions, we must grant that "God reveals Himself" both to Christian faith and to non-Christian faith, but that "the thought and language" in which God is apprehended and interpreted are "always defective, sometimes gravely distorting".

At the level of dogma, rite, myth, institution and cult which comprise the religious complex, Kraemer is right in emphasizing that every religion should be seen as a totality, integrated, or being in the process of being integrated, on its own axis, and that the axes of Christianity and Hinduism are certainly antithetical. There is also validity in the classification of religions into prophetic religions of revelation and naturalistic religions of transempirical realization. But as there is divine self-revelation in non-Christian faith behind the religions, such classification has only relative validity.

Thus Hogg sees a real continuity between Christian faith and non-Christian faith and a real discontinuity between Christian religion and non-Christian religions. While there can be no direct fulfilment of other religions in Christianity, it may not be impossible to speak of Christian faith fulfilling the non-Christian faith. Here he sees also the relevance of the Christian mission.

Hogg affirms that in India, where he has worked as a missionary for many years, he had "known" and "had fellowship" with some for whom Christ was not absolute Lord and only Saviour, and who held typically Hindu beliefs but "yet manifestly were no strangers to life 'hid in God'". If experience of Christ is newness, many a Hindu who has attained "realization" of God, whether by the more theistic or the more monistic path, has testified to such newness.

Of course the whole church is under a great debt to Barthian theology for emphasizing the uniqueness of the spiritual verities of Romans 1-8, the releasing power of justification by faith alone and of the new life in Christ Jesus. But even Christian life may begin with less mature experiences. Often it is the "fellowship with Christ as he daily bears for us whatever is our felt burden that gradually moulds us into a likeness to Him which makes our burdens change their quality". If there is continuity between the immature and mature experiences of Christ, is it valid to affirm "an absolute discontinuity" between faith that is typically Christian and faith that is still apart from Christ?

What Matthew 11:27 affirms is that it is only through Jesus that humanity comes to know God as "Father"; it does not say that "except through him no one can come to 'God'". It is the Father-child relationship that is uniquely the religious life which Jesus gives. Hogg interprets the "only Saving name" verse of Acts 4:12 to mean that it is only because of Jesus and the cross that we know the graciousness of God transcending religions.

Here Hogg naturally raises the question of the church's mission of conversion. If there are high levels of spiritual life in other religions, "why should Christian effort be directed towards getting them to change their religion instead of to make progress within the religion they already profess?" The answer is to be found in the ultimate goal towards which God is leading all humanity and the educational enterprise in which God is engaged in order to realize it. God is "the kind of Father who longs to make of his human children little comrades and is even taking the initiative towards this end". This purpose was first apprehended by the people of Israel, who were educated through the prophets in the costliness of "the blessedness of being chosen for fellowship with a Divine Comrade". It was through Israel that "the great concepts" of the world's Creation and Fall, of a Messianic Age, and a Messianic King, a Suffering Servant, Resurrection, and Son of Man, came into the history of religion. They became "the vessels into which God was able to pour his supreme revelation when he sent his Son into the world". The biblical revelation is thus the Divine Father leading humanity to adult sonship. And Hogg considers it "unfaithful" to this revelation if the emphasis on "Divine Majesty and Infinitude" is allowed to cloud it. This is Hogg's criticism of the Barthian emphasis on divine sovereignty to the point of weakening God's parental concern for humankind.

More importantly, Hogg takes the example of the human parent entering into communion with the child in different ways at different stages of the child's growth from infancy to adulthood. This for him is a parable of God-humanity relations. The parent has communion with the infant even when there is no possibility of "spoken intercourse". He asks: "Can the fatherly love of the Creator be deemed to have denied itself all means of making to primitive man the degree of self-disclosure which the mother makes to her infant by corporal fondling, checking, tending?" There is divine revelation in the sense of the numinous awakened in the primitive. This may puzzle our philosophy, but it is "as certain as that God is active love".

At the stage of the spoken intercourse, there is "parental disclosure in words" that falls short of or even misconstrues the truth. Similarly the Father helps the human soul to understand "the purpose of his will partly in ways that are crude and in many ways far astray". This too is self-disclosure. At the time of a young person's schooling and his/her emergence into self-direction, the parent assists in the self-unfolding. Later comes the further education of a conceptual nature. So also God's pedagogy. "If God is to be the self-revealer, he has also to be the teacher, whose constant aim is to evoke in the human soul the right kind of seeking." And Hogg interprets in this light the plurality of religions and the preparation of Israel for the incarnation. He says:

> Part of the meaning of human history up to the Incarnation was that in it God was developing the kind of human concepts (e.g. the Hebrew concepts of the kingdom of God, the Messiah, the Supernatural Son of Man and Suffering Servant and the Greek concept of the Logos) that would enable men to apprehend conceptually, without a radical degree of distortion, his perfect expression of himself towards our race in the medium of action and personality. It was in the Mediterranean world that this conceptual development came to function.

The conceptual development of religion in India followed a very different direction, so that the human apprehension of God's eternal activity of self-expression suffered a "grievous distortion". This explains "why when the Word was made flesh this took place in the Mediterranean world". But that does not mean that "the Word did not come to India at all" or that there was no revelation.

Hogg sums up his argument:

> Where Christ has not yet been spiritually apprehended there may be other ways than He to the trust in God which enables our Heavenly Father to bestow on a man some measure of communion with Himself. But when Christ succeeds in unveiling for any man the judgment of God on sin, in this very act

> He cannot help making Himself, for that man, the one and only way. Christ is the only way to God that can remain permanently a thoroughfare.

Here, as a missionary engaged in education, Hogg sees the role of "the winds of intellectual and cultural progress" in spiritual awakening. Intellectual and cultural changes alter the shape of the problems of life to be encountered and make traditional doctrines opaque to further light of God. At this point, Christianity may have "the privilege of enabling those who, without clear understanding, have held so tightly to Him, to win far ahead of us in intimacy of fellowship".

Finally Hogg criticizes Kraemer for not distinguishing between the "occurrence" and the "content" of revelation. This point is taken up by D.G. Moses in his study of Kraemer's position.[31] He quotes Hogg and says that "Christianity is unique because of the unique 'content' of the revelation of which it is the apprehension and product and to which it bears witness. And that content must win conviction by its own direct appeal by its illuminating and renovating power" without depending for its truth merely on a subjective assertion of the believer that he or she is communicating an objective revelation.

According to Moses, this approach will better account for the great moral and religious insights and the good and beautiful lives in the non-Christian religions. It will also make Kraemer's criterion of truth "less authoritarian" and more objective.

Incarnation, a birth and not a bomb: P. Chenchiah

Chenchiah's review of Kraemer's book in *Rethinking Christianity in India*[32] begins with a criticism of Kraemer's Barthian standpoint.

His basic thrust is that in Barth's theology God's revelation in Jesus Christ not only transcends history but also remains transcendentalist; that is, remains outside history without entering it to fulfill the divine purpose for the created order. "The possibility of God permanently entering the creative order is not favoured by Barth, his crucial idea being that God always operates on creation 'vertically' on men by 'crisis'."

This, Chenchiah is convinced, is against the theology underlying the doctrine of the incarnation in the Fourth Gospel, and even opposed to the doctrine of the Person of the Holy Spirit dwelling in human beings in St Paul's thought.

Chenchiah's criticism is centred on his protest against the idea of God as Absolute and Kraemer's jehad against Relativism in God's name. That protest is in the name of Jesus as the "human God". He says: "Relativists may renounce the 'absolute' God but do not for that reason forego God altogether. The finite God is still God, yea, even so our Lord Jesus Christ." He strongly opposes the inference that those who have lost faith in the absolute have lost faith altogether in God. "Who is to judge between the theologian's Absolute and man's human God?"

The Absolute of the philosophy as expounded by Sankara, Kant and Bradley is unconditioned, unrelated and changeless. Even when converted into "religious Absolute" as in India, it has been difficult to recognize personal reality in God and the significance of human history for God. Though Barthians are thinking of a moral absolute as opposed to the metaphysical, it does not alter the situation. In his comments on a later consultation with Kraemer in India, Chenchiah opposes the idea of the Absolute, common to Kraemer and Radhakrishnan, in spite of their deep differences.

> There is a humorous side to this Barthian-Advaitic Kraemer-Radhakrishnan duel. Both believe in the Absolute. Both discard relativism, one as sin and the other as maya. I am a relativist and don't believe in the Absolute, whatever it may mean. I have a right to pick a bone with these. Why these blood brothers quarrel I don't know. I believe the Absolute a construct of the mind. The Absolute is metaphysical while the Relative is historical.[33]

The malady of modern societies is not relativism as Kraemer argues. And the solution to the malady is "not an absolute in heaven but a power greater than we on earth", Emmanuel, God with us.

Chenchiah sees "very little" of the absolute in the Old Testament Yahweh; and certainly herein lies "the supreme excellence of Jesus" who is the critique of the Absolute.

> Our Lord is the true measure of the criticism of the Absolute. In his presence we feel the "relation" of God to us — his nearness and intimacy — rather than his absoluteness, his unattainability. Jesus is not God the Absolute but God as standing in relation to man — not God who operates vertically and in crisis. The meeting of God and Jesus and his disciples, though critical, was never a crisis ultimately. The harmony and intimacy of the relationship between God, Jesus and sons of God repels Barthian adjectives.[34]

Here Chenchiah's rejection of the Barth-Kraemer idea of the absolute God, and even more the absolute Jesus, is total. It is in the relation of God to human history that Jesus has made a revolution. If Judaism spoke of God as a person permanently residing in heaven and occasionally visiting the earth, the incarnation affirms that "God is not only coming to us occasionally but is born among us". And Christianity holds that if Christ has gone to heaven, "the Holy Spirit comes down in his stead" to reside permanently with us. Christianity permanently changes the residence of God. God as "our Father in heaven" may still be true:

> But we have to speak of the Holy Spirit that resides in us and with us and of Christ who has gone up only to come back again. This differs radically from Barth's God touching us without touching, that is, as the tangent touches the circle. Far from touching, he breaks into history and abides with us.

Chenchiah takes up Kraemer's fivefold definition of the gospel — as Incarnation, Justification, Reconciliation and Atonement, Movement of the Kingdom of God, and New Way — and points to its lopsidedness, precisely because the Barthian idea of revelation he adopts is too tangential to human history and cosmic process.

> The Incarnation has its spearhead towards creation. To turn it round and make it face heaven is to reverse its purpose.... Jesus is not God and is not Man, but is the Son of Man. The word "Son" indicates the measure of unity between God, Jesus and the Christian... India will not be afraid of claiming Jesus as belonging to our race as the head of humanity, as the Son of Man. This is the message of Christianity, that the Word has become flesh and God has become man... Jesus then is not a bomb, but a birth, not a tangent but the radius.[35]

But what does this "birth" mean? For Chenchiah it means that in Jesus the creative process of human and cosmic evolution reaches a new stage, discontinuous with all the past. There is a New Creation. Not only the individual human being but the whole human species and the cosmos together move on to the Future which is the kingdom of God. Here, of course, Chenchiah is critical of theologians who see Jesus as "restoring" the human being to an original sinless paradise. For him, the restoration is only to enable a new beginning.

> What can we say to the Gospel which limits the totality of Christ's achievement to a restoration of man to the original condition? This restoration and reconciliation can only be the new start for life and not its positive content. Is there any advance for man in Jesus beyond regaining the ground lost? One must confess that Dr Kraemer touches rather gingerly the positive aspects of Christ. The Incarnation in its significance for the destiny of man; the Kingdom of God as a new world order to be evolved out of the present existence; the Holy Spirit as the new cosmic energy — receive rather disappointing treatment, possibly by reason of the Barthian theology adopted.

Here is a comparison between the Barthian and Hindu views of incarnation which is very significant. Chenchiah says that the Barthian view is “akin to the Hindu view”. “For in Hinduism God incarnates when the constitution of the world is threatened, and comes not to be with us always but to restore the mechanism of life to its original condition. One should have thought that the Christian conception is something more than this.”

> ...the fact of Christ is the birth of a new order of creation. It is the emergence of life — not bound by *karma*; of man not tainted by sin, not humbled by death; of man triumphant, glorious, partaking the immortal nature of God; of the birth of a new race, of the creation of the sons of God. If Jesus is not the incarnation of this, what else could he be? Is he not Emmanuel, God permanently residing in the creation — the answer to the prayer of man to transcend his destiny? If the Incarnation is the answer to our ambition and not to our infirmities — then humanity has a future, a new future more in accord with its aspirations.[36]

The incarnation is here related by Chenchiah to the “ambition” of human creativity and maturity. Jesus is the Son of God through whom “we can be and ought to be sons of God now and here — not in the far off future” or somewhere else. Chenchiah rejects the idea of the kingdom descending “from heaven when Christ comes” as a heresy because it removes the kingdom from the historical present and future of humanity.

This does not mean that for Chenchiah the kingdom of God is the end-product of a self-sufficient process. He rejects the view that the higher is “merely a fuller expression of the lower”: he rejects also that the higher “does not continue the old”. Just as man is “not a perfect animal” but transcends the animal, Jesus is “not perfected man; he transcends man” — “without sin, without stain, without inner strife... without decay and death”. Adds Chenchiah:

> But for all this, he is the new man — man without *karma*. You cannot and should not detach him from the claim of humanity and throw him back into the eternal mystery beyond creation. The Kingdom of God is a new world order, expressing a new cosmic power — the Holy Spirit.

This, he says, is the difference between the kingdom of God and scientific humanist utopias. The transcendent power of the Holy Spirit takes religion and science in its embrace and builds the new humanity. A Christianity in which “God, Jesus, the Kingdom of God hover over man and the world, attracting us but never touching our world order or even becoming part of it” is not true to Jesus.

The exaggerated transcendentalism of the kingdom in Barth and Kraemer prevents the transcendent power of Jesus and the Spirit from being and becoming the dynamic of the historical process. This is responsible for Kraemer's rejection of the Sermon on the Mount as impractical.

It is on the basis of this critique of Barth-Kraemer Christology that Chenchiah rejects Kraemer's theology of the relation between revelation and religions. He notes that Kraemer rejects both Aquinas's blend of natural theology and Christian revelation and Barth's refusal to enter into the question of general revelation. Chenchiah agrees with Kraemer on these, but considers Kraemer's own alternative disappointing. He avoids the real question. "What we have to answer is whether God has dealt with man in the past and if He has, have His dealings any bearing on Christian revelation?"

Chenchiah accepts Kraemer's thesis that each religion is a totality around its own axis. It is futile to understand the relation between religions as though the several religions answer the same question. Every religion is "a circle complete and perfect in itself". The theory of equality of all religions is no more than "a token of good will". But the real question is whether God has given to other religions the saving knowledge of God's own being. And Chenchiah thinks that Kraemer's devotion to "doctrine" — which Kraemer criticizes in Barth — blinds him from seeing that "reconciliation and redemption are part of the general revelation accomplished by God in many ways in history".

This does not mean that the "special revelation" in Jesus is a continuation of the general revelation in any religion, Judaic or Hindu. "The special revelation lies in the creative progress of life in Jesus." Jesus as the New Man is new to and discontinuous with all religions.

> It is by no means easy to discover elements in other faiths which find fulfilment in Jesus. When these elements are found out, it will be seen they do not receive any great emphasis in Hinduism... Jesus kindles new hopes not felt, and kills some of the deepest and persistent longings of man. In this region, "fulfilment" has no relevance. Nevertheless, if Christianity is the summation of the creative process we should expect tendencies and processes spread all over the religious field pointing towards the expected advent of a new age. As the prophets foresaw what was to come, the seers and the saints also must have had pre-vision of the Redemption to come.

That is to say, Jesus is "the 'new given' that has entered the world" and stands as new creation to the old, continuous with it without transcending it. So, as one deeply drawing spiritual sustenance from his Hindu tradition but as one having found something radically new in Jesus, Chenchiah says:

Hinduism makes the perfect man, Christianity the New Man. Hinduism harnesses the *Mahasakti* of nature and man, Christianity brings into evolution the New *Sakti* of the Holy Spirit. Jesus is the first fruits of a New Creation. Hinduism is the final fruit of the old creation.[38]

Therefore the interaction between Christianity and Hinduism should happen within the framework of the need of Indian Christianity to recover the Hindu heritage and of understanding the newness of Christ in relation to that heritage and the future of Hinduism and India. The dream of Hinduism is of a life not subject to the limitations of decay. For this it has in the past pressed into its service all the resources of power available in creation. But the secret of perpetual life is not in creation. The age-long effort for new life bears fruit only when it brings into creation an energy from beyond, an energy which can lift humankind above itself. "It is the claim of Christianity that in Jesus such an energy has entered into creation."[37]

4. A dialectical theology of secularism

The Barth-Brunner-Kraemer interpretation of Revelation over against Religion has had two lines of development in ecumenical circles.

The first line is that of seeing Christianity as the only true divinely chosen religion among the religions of humankind, because it alone is open to the judging and therefore redeeming grace of God's revelation in Jesus Christ. As we have seen, Karl Barth and even more aggressively Hendrick Kraemer build their theology of Christian mission along this line.

However, there is another line which may be taken as post-Barthian and post-Kraemerian. It bases itself on Barth's negative evaluation of all religions in the light of revelation, but it rejects the transcendentalism characteristic of his doctrine of Revelation. Along this line, it interprets the movement of the secularization of cultures, and even some forms of atheism, as the result of the impact of the Christian gospel, and explores the possibility of divine grace taking "historical form" in a radical secular Christianity. The writings of Dietrich Bonhoeffer and A.T. van Leeuwen are typical of this theological approach. Says John Carman:

In this view the true form of Christian faith is devoid of religion and indeed in fundamental opposition to religion. From the time of the Hebrew prophets onwards, true faith has shown its opposition to human religion, but now in our time it is possible to rid faith completely of the trappings of religion and proclaim a completely secular gospel for modern people.[39]

This has been a major ecumenical trend in the post-war theology of religion.

Religionless Christianity for a world come of age: Dietrich Bonhoeffer

It was in his *Letters and Papers from Prison* that Dietrich Bonhoeffer suggested the possibility of a religionless Christianity for a world come of age. He saw it as a development from Barth's ideas of revelation as the abolition of religion. It was, however, a development critical of what he called Barth's "positivism of revelation".

By "positivism of revelation" in Barth, Bonhoeffer seems to mean more or less what Hogg meant when he criticized Kraemer for ignoring the "content" of the revelation in his preoccupation with its "occurrence". According to Bonhoeffer, Barth has reduced revelation to "data (*posita*)... to be accepted without any further elucidation".[40]

The important question for Bonhoeffer is "what Christianity actually is or who Christ really is for us today". "Today" is the crucial word. Through the Renaissance and the Enlightenment, human beings have secured control over nature and society and have become aware of being responsible for their historical destiny. This is what Bonhoeffer means by the world's coming of age or humanity's growth to adulthood. In this context, much of the old forms of religion, including those of Christianity, which were expressions of human immaturity, have become irrelevant and meaningless. Bonhoeffer speaks of various forms of religion and belief in God which make little sense to the modern secular world. In one letter he says that in prison he shrinks from speaking of God by name with religious people, because "that name somehow here seems to me not to ring true". He adds:

> Religious people speak of God when human perception is (often from laziness) at an end or human resources fail; it is really always the *deus ex machina* they call to their aid, either for the solving of insolvable problems or as support in human failure... Of necessity that can only go on until men can, by their own strength, push these borders back a little further, so that God becomes superfluous as a *deus ex machina*.[41]

The truth about modern societies is that they have "learned to cope with all questions of importance without recourse to God as a working hypothesis". And the crucial question for the church is whether we can talk of God "not on the borders of existence but at its centre, not in weakness but in strength, not therefore in man's suffering and death but in his life and prosperity". Can God be "the Beyond in the midst of our life"?

What Bonhoeffer asks for is a theological understanding of the maturity of modern secularized human beings and the meaning of Christian faith for their life. It is here that Bonhoeffer is drawn to Karl Barth's idea of revelation as abolition of religion. He admits that Barth is the first theologian to provide a radical critique of religion, thus opening up the possibility of speaking about Christ to the secular humanity of our times about the meaning of "true worldliness". But he finds that Barth's doctrine of revelation cannot relate meaningfully to the secularity of modern adult humanity because of its "positivism". That is, for Barth revelation is to declare certain dogmas as objectively revealed truths from God, without bothering to elucidate their meaning for the modern world. It is to say: "Take it or leave it — virgin birth, trinity or anything else, everything which is an equally significant and necessary part of the whole, which has to be swallowed as a whole or not at all."

With this criticism, Bonhoeffer attempts to outline the post-Barthian theology of the world come of age. He does so by reinterpreting the revelation of God in terms of the transcendent quality of humanness as "Man for others", of the Person of the Incarnate and Crucified Jesus Christ and concretely manifested in history in the fellowship of persons.

In a survey of the history of Bonhoeffer's thought from his early writings to the prison letters and papers, Bethge says that from the very beginning revelation for Bonhoeffer had the character of historical concreteness. In *Act and Being*[42] Bonhoeffer affirms that "God is not free of man, but *for* man; and Christ is the word of his freedom. God is there, which is to say, not in eternal non-objectivity, but have-able, graspable in his word within the church." For Barth, Divine Majesty seems to necessitate "pushing God away" from the world, but for Bonhoeffer it lies in "drawing him in". Bonhoeffer finds the fullness of God in "that limited weak and humiliated man Jesus, who took the risk of utter human concreteness". In his *Ethics*,[43] Bonhoeffer sees in Jesus Christ the unity of the ultimate and the penultimate without destroying the autonomy of the penultimate; in fact the penultimate has "become the outer covering for the ultimate" and life in the penultimate becomes "participation in the encounter of Christ with the world". Thus incarnation neither destroys the worldly reality nor converts it into Christendom, but enables human beings to live humanly before God. The cross of Jesus in particular destroys all idolatries in the world, thereby revealing and renewing "true worldliness, true this-worldliness and true godlessness" under God.

Thus for Bonhoeffer, the Renaissance and the Enlightenment and their affirmation of the world's autonomy from religion, and even from God, relatively speaking, are a fruit of the divine revelation in Jesus Christ. It is part of the Christian heritage and Christianity should take a "religionless" form to recognize it as Christian heritage. This is necessary also to save the modern world from the demonism of a secularism reduced to idolatry. Christianity is not an end in itself; the mission of the church is to present Christ as upholding humanity come of age.

Karl Barth considered Bonhoeffer's criticism of his doctrine as "positivism of revelation" and the thesis of "religionless" Christianity as unclear and enigmatic. Indeed, there is a lack of clarity. But the picture of Jesus as the revelation of God suffering in "being for others" and the definition of transcendence as "participation in the being of Jesus for others in the world" are clear enough. So also is the understanding of the mission of the church of Christ as that of enabling secularized modern humanity to live a life of true secularity in the world and to exercise the tragic responsibilities of autonomy with the knowledge of being justified and upheld by faith in Christ.

In Bonhoeffer's prison letters and papers, he says that as the "man for others and hence the crucified", Jesus is "God in human form". Faith is the "participation in this being of Jesus" in the world. Our relation to God need not take the "religious" form of being related to "some supreme almighty best of all beings"; rather it is "a new life in being there for others in participation in the being of Jesus". Contrasted with the false transcendence of religion, true transcendence is "an event which happens to us", given to us in Christ when we are "confronted by the other, by the accessible neighbour who is given to us again and again".

Bonhoeffer describes in the language of paradox the hidden presence of God in the life lived non-religiously without God in the modern world:

> God gives us to know that we must live as men who manage our lives without God. The God who is with us is the God *who* forsakes us (Mark 15:34). The God who lets us live in the world without the working hypothesis of God is the God before whom we are ever standing. Before God and with God we live without God.

This is possible without falling into idolatries of religion or secularism because of the revelation of God in the powerlessness and weakness of the crucified Jesus. Says Bonhoeffer: "God lets himself be drawn out of the world on to the Cross. God is powerless and weak in the world, and that is precisely the way, the only way, in which he is with us, and helps us.

Matthew 8:17... makes clear that Christ does not help in virtue of his omnipotence but by his weakness and suffering."

Perhaps the following formulation of Bonhoeffer's thought on the question of Christ and religions is even more telling:

> How can Christ become Lord even of those with no religion? If religion is no more than the garment of Christianity — and even that garment has had very different aspects at different periods — then what is a religionless Christianity?... What is the significance of a Church ... in a religionless world? ... In what way are we in a religionless and secular sense Christians... not conceiving of ourselves religiously as specially favoured, but as wholly belonging to the world? Then Christ is no longer an object of religion, but something quite different, indeed and in truth the Lord of the World.[44]

Secularism: ally of Christianity against religion: Arend van Leeuwen

Secularization as the fruit of the gospel and secularism as an ally of Christianity in the struggle against religion — that is the theme of Arend van Leeuwen's book *Christianity in World History*.[45]

It is significant that Kraemer writes a foreword commending the book to Western Christian missions. Indeed the thesis that the world mission of Western secular technological civilization has a unique character, arising from its relation to prophetic Christianity, and has a unique vocation in revolutionizing the religious cultures of Asia and Africa, is an extension into the cultural sphere of Kraemer's thesis in the *Christian Message in a Non-Christian World*. But van Leeuwen goes beyond Kraemer because his primary interest is in exploring the dialectics of the relation between biblical realism expressed in the missionary exansion of Western Christianity and biblical realism manifested in the global outreach of modern Western civilization.

Van Leeuwen rightly affirms that the emergence of independent Asian-African nations only deepens the cultural penetration of the West in their societies, for "the non-western countries which have achieved independence are certainly implementing a programme of Westernization". But in most cases, van Leeuwen observes, it goes with an open aversion to Christianization. This is evidenced in the resurgence of ancient religions and the opposition to Christian missions.

Thus it raises the question of the relation between the Christianity which they reject and the modern technology and secular culture which they welcome. Van Leeuwen asks: "Is it not precisely within the bosom of Christianity itself that this divorce — or distinction — between Western civilization and Christian faith has come about? And does it not in fact rest on the presupposition of Christian thinking? Is not the process of emancipation from religious restraints, which is usually referred to as secularization, itself a product of Western Christian civilization, and has it not been nurtured in the course of Christian history?"

Van Leeuwen's answer to these questions is an emphatic yes. It is an affirmation that behind Western civilization and all its technical and cultural products lies "the dynamic spirit of Christianity". It means then that that spirit is active now in the non-Western societies "in the guise of secularism, *incognito* so to speak". And maybe in that guise Christianity has entered a new phase of its history in which it presents itself no longer in the form of a self-centred *corpus Christianum* but in the form of "a victorious secularized civilization". Van Leeuwen calls upon the missionary movement to recognize this and build the strategy of Christian ecumenism on the basis that the secular ferment in the religious cultures of the East bears the seed of the Christian gospel.

From this angle, he interprets the emergence and spread of modern secular civilization "within the total setting of Christian history". To overemphasize the distinction between a "Christian" antiquity and the Middle Ages and a "secularized" modern period is to distort the fact that the latter in one sense is not a negation but a fulfilment of the former. This also implies giving up the popular distinction between the "materialist" West and the "spiritual" East and the advocacy of East-West dialogue on that basis. Rather we must discern, in the encounter of Western secularism with Eastern religious cultures, a setting in which the East inevitably gets involved in "the circumstances and decisions of Western history and therefore finds itself confronted willy-nilly with the choice to which world history leads, the choice which the future holds for East and West alike: the choice between Christ and Anti-Christ, annihilation and the risen Lord."

The starting point and the basic pattern of the encounter of the secular with the totalitarianism of religion is that of "Israel and the nations" in the Bible, the struggle of the prophetic tradition against the religions of the civilizations of the Near and Middle East. Van Leeuwen defines them as "ontocratic", that is, based on an apprehension of reality as cosmic totality with state and society manifesting the sacred order. Against this, the vision of Israel was that of the Creator-God breaking the human-made unity of the Tower of Babel and of the coming of God as King in history (eschatology). Within its "theocentric" approach, culture, society and state acquired a provisional and secular character. Indeed the struggle between theocratic and ontocratic patterns of life could be understood as the struggle between God and religion. An eschatological dimension is thus given to history. It is continued in a new way in the New Testament which sees in the incarnation, the cross and the resurrection of Jesus the first fruits of the kingdom of God — as both judgment on and fulfilment of a universal history. The theocratic pattern is continued through Christianity as it moves from the Jews to the Greeks and to the barbarians.

Van Leeuwen shows how in medieval Europe the conflict of church and state "ended by depriving the state of its sacral character". Medieval Christendom had to break up because "it proved impossible to build a truly Christian order along an ontocratic pattern". In fact, "the key to the extraordinary dynamic nature of medieval western history is not the struggle between King and Priest; it lies rather with the judgment that falls alike on throne and altar. Beneath the surface of things rages the conflict between heaven and earth, theocracy and ontocracy, the kingdom of the Lord and the power of man, the spirit and the flesh."

Science and technology provide the best example of "the radical break of the West" with the ontocratic pattern. It looks as though the whole course of Western history "has been leading towards this climax and fulfilment". Greek science had made its contribution, but Greek logos could not have become modern science without the Christian doctrine of creation which "freed (it) from all metaphysics and myths" to consider the immediate experience of the empirical world as a path to truth. Behind the scientific attitude lies the belief that the world is God's creation, redeemed into the new creation in Christ. "The Bible proclaims the logos incarnate, crucified and resurrected the first fruit of a new creation. The cosmos is not itself in the perfect form which the Greeks imagined it to be, but the creation in travail, reaching out towards redemption." The full significance of the technological revolution, says van Leeuwen, can only be grasped in "the context of the overall development which goes by the name of secularization" understood biblically as emancipation from the power of religion as ontocracy. It was such an emancipation which happened when the "sacred kingship" of Israel was destroyed, the temple brought down and the holy people scattered among the nations. It reaches its climax at the cross where "God's judgment is passed upon the Messiah of Israel, upon God's own appointed Son". It continues in the church's freedom from the "tyranny of the Hellenistic deification of the state"; and in the end the Christendom which the church built "collapses from within under the impact of forces which the church herself has stirred into active life... Christianization and secularization are thus involved together in a dialectical relation".

According to van Leeuwen, the East, unlike the West, never broke with the ontocratic pattern until it was challenged by its meeting with the West. The challenge has come to Asia and Africa not only or even primarily through Western Christianity but through the many material, intellectual and cultural goods from the West. The response varies, but insofar as nationalism and nation-building in Asia and Africa are absorbing the demythologization of religion, the secularization of the state, society and culture, the spirit of science and technology and the concept of individual person, ontocracy is shaken to its foundations by the new ethos. And there is no going back. It is in this new phase of Western civilization that Christianity has to rethink its mission.

In the final chapter of the book, entitled "Christianity in a Planetary World," van Leeuwen speaks of the new revolution taking place through the impact of technology. Its newness lies not only in its material aspects, but also in its capacity to "uproot and destroy" the religious cornerstone of societies. "For the first time in the history of mankind... the ontocractic pattern has been broken through and superseded by the technocratic pattern." In this, Christianity is in one sense dealing with its own child, however rebellious. For other religions and cultures it is a strange new reality.

Van Leeuwen discusses the approach of the Jerusalem 1928 and Tambaram 1938 world missionary conferences to the "rapidly increasing secularism" engulfing the modern world. The Jerusalem suggestion that "Christianity should form a common front with the other religions" against secularism, according to him, misinterprets the theological issue. "The technocratic era, though it is not the kingdom of God, is not the kingdom of Satan either; it is a phase of history in which the Lord and Satan are both at work." The church cannot now return to the age of "religion". Nor is it the issue that "the non-Western world can be or ought to be 'Christianized' in the sense that the traditional non-Western religions would in the long run give place to Christianity in some version or other of the corpus Christianum".

Van Leeuwen is critical of the Tambaram 1938 discussions, following Kraemer's book. To him they "illustrated clearly to what extent the church has confined her outlook on the missionary task of the 'religious' dimension". To save the technological revolution, what is required is another revolution which will release here and now, in our planetary and technocratic world, "recreative forces like those which burst their way through the religious world of the West in the Renaissance, the Reformation and the subsequent movements". He sees signs of an awakening of this kind in the theologies of Karl Barth and Dietrich Bonhoeffer.

Christianity, says Van Leeuwen, "should risk facing the hazardous encounter with the very 'atheism' and 'nihilism' which the preaching of the gospel has itself produced. That is the needle's eye through which the theology of the twentieth century must pass if it is to enter the kingdom of God." The priority of the church in the West is with "the business of secularization and of our encounter with it"; and in the non-Western world priority lies in our relation to "the processes of rapid social change... and not in those areas where the traditions still maintain an uninterrupted life". It is here "at the base" and "not at the top" that the encounter between the Christian faith and the non-Christian religions must take place. That is to say, "it lies in the cooperation of Christians with non-Christians in a concerted effort to build ourselves a city and a tower" but without an over-arching "religious" top as with the Tower of Babel.

Where the impact of secularism has "made a breach in the totalitarian authority of the sacred tradition" and the "religious myth" has been blown away, the way is open for religions to bring to the task of building the new city treasures of great value from their traditions.

5. Christ of the movements of Renaissance

We have examined three major approaches in the missionary/ecumenical transactions with religious pluralism — the advocacy for a united front of religion against secularism (Hocking), the plea to present the uniqueness of Christianity as against other religions (Kraemer), and the suggestion to develop a Christian-secular united front against religion (van Leeuwen).

Among the churches and interchurch councils in the third world, however, there has evolved a theology of Christian partnership with non-Christian religions and secular ideologies involved in the struggle for new life for the people. This came out of years of reflection on the cultural renaissance which accompanied the political movements for national freedom, nation-building and social liberation, and sought to explore the spiritual foundations for the people's struggle. It involves, as Stanley Samartha has shown, an acknowledgment of the presence of Christ in "the movements of innovation", that is to say, in the renascent movements within various religions and new developments in certain ideologies, which have come up in the living context of people of various faiths as they were caught up in "an interdependent world struggle for renewal".[46]

Stanley J. Samartha

Among the movements of innovation of this nature which Samartha mentions are independent African movements which seek to draw on African cultural and spiritual resources for wholeness of life, the movements within Buddhism such as Rissho Kosei-Kai of Japan with their emphasis on lay people and on practical guidance to meet the problems of daily life, the renascence and resurgence of Islam which finds various manifestations in the Islamic world, the neo-Marxist movements, and, of course, neo-Hindu movements of Yoga, transcendental meditation and Krishna consciousness. All these seem to disprove the prophecies of those who predicted that religion would be swept away in the stream of modern life.

Samartha mentions several characteristics of the movements of innovation to show the spiritual vitality and the new direction which find expression in them. Firstly, there is the emphasis on "a fuller, more satisfying *human* life here and now", as in the revolution in China, Hoza in Japan, Ramakrishna mission in India. Secondly, they represent "the search for new forms of community", which recognize the pressures of modern life and do not embody the injustices of traditional societies. Thirdly, there is an emphasis on the individual human *person*, the meaning and destiny of personal life in the cosmic process and the vocation of the person in the community. Fourthly, all these movements "go back to the *spiritual core* of their respective faiths" to reinterpret themselves and interpret others. Fifthly, there is an "*inter-relation* between religious movements of innovation and ideological movements", though the exact nature of it is unclear. Samartha adds a special word here on "the significance of *China*" and the formidable spiritual force of the Chinese revolution — which C.S. Song describes as "a secularized version of salvation history".

Samartha's final point is that "the gospel itself, directly or indirectly, has been one of the factors in generating new movements". He says that the "gospel does produce a ferment even while it is being opposed or attacked or received with joy".

This raises the question of the interpretation of these movements of innovation in the light of Christ. Some approaches like those of Kraemer and van Leeuwen would consider such movements as opposed to Christ so long as the innovations at the level of human "values" are coupled with a hardening of the "spiritual core" of their traditional faiths. Samartha rejects this thesis. He rejects also the approach of "inclusivism" of two kinds. One of these puts the Christian label on others without their leave.

"Inclusivism without consent" can be, says Samartha, as patronizing as excluding others from the household of God. The other view which affirms that all movements of innovation "participate in the same mission of God in the world which we Christians distinctly understand as manifest in Jesus Christ" lacks a principle of discrimination. It is more discriminatory to say that all movements of innovation "which bear the marks of the ministry of Jesus Christ" are from the Holy Spirit. He asks whether, where there is a certain parallel or a convergence, there is any valid reason to ignore the parallelism or to reject cooperation.

> If we take seriously the implications of our faith, viz. that we believe in the *living* God, in Christ who is the Lord of *history*, including contemporary history, and in the promise that the Spirit will guide us into all truth, then can we deny that Christ is at work wherever people are struggling for freedom and renewal, seeking for fullness of life, peace and joy?... The struggle between newness of life and petrified tradition, between truth and distortions of truth, between God and the idols, is going on everywhere. It will be a mistake to regard it as a contest between Christianity and non-Christian religions or between Christ and atheistic ideologies.

Samartha ends the essay by cautioning Christians against too hasty negative judgments even about the "truth claims" and messages of "salvation" in other religions "on which the spiritual life of millions of our neighbours have been sustained over the centuries". In an interdependent world, where the search for renewal is a common quest, a shared search for all people, we must find out through patient dialogue what unites and what separates us at the deepest level. "Our hope lies in the continuing work of the Holy Spirit in judgment, mercy and new creation."

Towards a theology of Asian renaissance

As early as 1949, the Asian church leaders meeting in Bangkok, soon after Indian independence and the Chinese revolution, had observed the universality of the demand for cultural and social renewal in Asian societies. They had tried to interpret and respond to the search for fuller human life inherent in it.

The report of the meeting on the "Church in Social and Political Life"[47] notes the conditions of abject poverty in which the majority of people in rural and urban Asia live. It talks of their awakening to "a new sense of human dignity and historical mission". These, it says, are "basic elements in the revolutionary ferment" at work in Asia, leading to demands for change. It is a creative stage in Asian life, with possibilities for good and evil, for the discovery of the human person and responsible human community as well as for the rise of movements of nihilism and totalitarianism. "The Christian church must welcome the demand of the peoples for a fuller participation in the life of society at the level where power is exercised, since this is an expression of human dignity." Therefore, ideologies which have arisen to "interpret the revolution to the common man and to lead him in his search for his destiny" should be examined in the light of their capacity to promote justice and humanity. The report speaks of the churches' witness in China; it should aim at providing "a moral and religious foundation for the new sense of social freedom and economic justice among the people"; and in the other countries where "the possibility exists of transforming the social order democratically" the churches are to work for "a true social democracy".

> We must recognize... that democratic institutions and values divorced from their original Christian motive exist in a moral and religious vacuum and tend to break down. The Christian has the task of redefining and reinforcing these institutions and values in the light of the Christian faith, supplying a moral dynamic which they lack today.

The report points out that the corporate life and spiritual mission of the church in the national communities have special relevance. Only that which transcends morals, namely "the knowledge of the ultimate accountability of man and society to God and of the grace of God by which men being forgiven forgive one another" can be the basis of true human community. The church's central task therefore is to proclaim the word of God "with a profound sense of its relevance to the ideological and political conflicts" of Asia, and to be "truly a community of persons rooted in the word of God... worshipping congregations in which human worth and mutual responsibility are aknowledged and realized and from which love goes out in work of service to the neighbourhood". The statement affirms that "a true Christian congregation" in the midst of people is "the most effective prophetic witness to the divine righteousness in society".

At the inaugural assembly of the East Asia Christian Conference in Kuala Lumpur in 1958, the theological interpretation of the Asian "revolutionary ferment" was taken to a new stage. The report on "The Church's Involvement in Contemporary Asian Societies"[48] speaks of the nature of the gospel and the gospel view of modern Asian history.

The gospel which the church proclaims is the message of "redemption of the whole human race and of the whole created world"; in the death and resurrection of Jesus Christ God has reconciled "all things to himself" and the goal is to "unite all things in Christ". It is also "the gospel of the kingship of Christ over the world". Therefore, says the report:

> The meaning of world history, including that of modern Asian history, is to be discovered in that kingship, which today is hidden and will be revealed at the end of time. The church must endeavour to discern how Christ is at work in the revolution of contemporary Asia:
> — releasing new creative forces,
> — judging idolatry and false gods,
> — leading peoples to a decision for or against him, and
> — gathering to himself those who respond in faith to him,
> — in order to send them back to be witnesses to his kingship.
>
> The church must not only discern Christ in the changing life but be there in it, making his presence and lordship known. It is this that is the substance of the church's witness amidst social change in Asia today. It is our common conviction that the church should be full participant in the new life of Asia, if she is to be effective in witnessing to Jesus Christ as Lord and Saviour.

It was within this theological setting of the Asian churches that centres for the study of religions and society were established in different countries of Asia. These centres participated in a common study on "The Word of God and the Living Faiths of Men" under the auspices of the ecumenical organizations. A statement on the "Renaissance of Religion in the Context of Social and Cultural Change", prepared at the meeting of the directors of the various study centres in East Asia in 1961,[49] affirms the empirical fact that the religions of Asia are "living realities" and that their resources are being "directed towards the efforts for national reconstruction in the context of the total cultural transformation of Asian peoples". It points out that the striving for "human values" such as social justice, human rights and a better quality of life, is "supported by the rediscovery of these values in the religious traditions".

Thus, "the forces of the new age" have been real factors in "the awakening of ancient faiths to new life". Among these forces are the impact of modern science and technology, ideologies of secular liberalism and communism and the work of Christian missions and churches. The result has been that "the historical faiths of Asia have assimilated values and emphases from each other as well as from Christianity" and seek to provide "an adequate dynamic faith for modern Asian man" and indeed for the modern world.

The secularization of Asian societies is related in part to the search for a common culture in a multi-religious situation. National solidarity and a basis for common action demand a measure of dissociation of the cultural element from the religious. "A certain measure of secularization of culture is inherent in this process. This has been welcomed by some religious groups as making possible the recovery of the true meaning of religion and its relation to secular life; such groups are making attempts to evolve a new secularism with a religious motivation." It stands alongside the secularism which opposes all religions. Other religious groups seek to "reassert the old religio-cultural unity as the only basis for national wholeness". This has led some Asian nations to proclaim the majority religion as a state religion. Christian communities of Asia are beginning to dissociate the Christian faith from Western culture and to "identify themselves increasingly with the culture of their own countries" and to establish their kinship with their own people.

All this involves a process of growing in self-understanding and self-esteem integral to "national selfhood"; and it embraces not only the intellectual but also the popular religion at various levels. And the Asian religious renaissance is closely related to the Asian social revolution.

What are some of the elements common to the renaissance taking place in all religions? First, a new emphasis on "common humanity", of peoples called together to confront the problems of common human existence. Second, "in all religions there is a new recognition of the worth and dignity of the human person" in relation to other persons constituting society, and to the rights to participate responsibly in making the decisions which make history. And third, a rejection of resignation in favour of "a new activism which draws on religious resources and finds expression in collective endeavour to realize new goals".

The statement points out that the "rediscovery of our common humanity" as the basis of common action has come about in each religion on the basis of its own faith. Therefore, it has also brought about an emphasis on the fundamental differences at the core of the different religions. It is noted that "in some instances the core seems to be growing harder and more distinctive", a situation which calls for "a new kind of dialogue" between Christians and others on the "nature and destiny of man", which has both ultimate and penultimate dimensions.

The directors of study centres assert that a Christian theology of inter-religious relations "should not remain entangled in theoretical alternatives such as continuity and discontinuity or general and special revelation". Its starting point should be "the biblical message that as God is the Creator of all men, so is his salvation in Jesus Christ offered to all men and that in him there is a new creation". The statement continues:

> God has called his church to be among men, the community of witnesses to his salvation and his kingdom. In various ways, through the religious and secular movements of our time, he is preparing the people to discern the true meaning of the offer of salvation in Christ and to face the decision for or against him.

This is the meaning of modern Asian history and the church must be fully present in it, responding to God in it, as witness to his kingdom. Not because Christians have any superiority in religion, metaphysics or spiritual self-liberation, but only because the church is "called to be obedient". But the "forms of religious expression" of that obedience must at their deepest level be "an expression of our common humanity".

How do Christians relate "the new solidarity which is found in our common humanity" across religious and secular faiths to the uniqueness of God's revelation in Jesus Christ? There are differences of approach at this point — some discerning the redemptive activity of God in other faiths and some only God's forbearance. But there is agreement on the need to work towards a new definition of the theological significance of other religions.

> In the contemporary religious situation, we find men of other faiths as well as secularists of many persuasions earnestly seeking for a new personal understanding of the meaning of life amidst the revolutionary scientific and technological transformations of life in Asia. We are forbidden to minimize the human values which are emerging through the renaissance of religions... We believe that God, as he has been active in all history since creation, is active in the religious changes of our time. In the light of these changes, the theological significance of the religions should be defined in a new way.

In 1966, when the East Asia Christian Conference had its Faith and Order consultation in Hongkong, on the topic of a "confessing church in Asia", it was urged that we "discern a special task of theology in relation to the Asian Renaissance and Revolution because we believe God is working out his purposes" in them.[50] Further, while Asian churches have inherited the "Great Tradition" of the universal gospel, "Christ has more of his truth to reveal to us as we seek to understand his work among men in their several Asian cultures, their different Asian religions, and their involvement in the contemporary Asian revolution." In the past Asian churches have been too inhibited by an idolatrous absolutization of inherited historical confessional formulations and by "our fear of syncretism" to make such ventures of confessing Christ "in our time and culture".

> A living theology must speak to the actual questions men in Asia are asking in the midst of their dilemmas, their hopes, aspirations and achievements, their doubts, despair and suffering. It must also speak in relation to the answers that are being given by Asian religions and philosophies, both in their classical forms and in new forms created by the impact on them of Western thought, secularism and science.[51]

Jesus Christ the new humanity

The Rapid Social Change Studies of the period between Evanston (1954) and New Delhi (1961), and the studies and events leading to the World Conference on Church and Society in Geneva (1966) on "Christians in the Technical and Social Revolutions of Our Time" made the ecumenical theological world conscious of the universal character of the search for human community on a new basis, and of the worldwide awakening of the poor and the oppressed for justice and humanity. There was also the awareness of the need of a Christology and an ecclesiology which could make human values integral to the ultimate human destiny. In certain respects the Uppsala Assembly in 1968 was a response to this new awareness.

Uppsala, in its report on "Renewal in Mission"[52] begins by acknowledging that Christians "belong to a humanity that cries passionately and articulately for a full human life" in situations in which destructive forces threaten its realization. Therefore, there is a burning relevance today in describing the mission of God, in which we participate, as the gift of a new creation which is a radical renewal of the old and the "invitation" to people to grow into their full humanity in the man Jesus Christ".

The Christological statement touched on here is explained thus:

> Jesus Christ, incarnate, crucified and risen, is the new man. In him was revealed the image of God as he glorified his Father in perfect obedience. In his total availability for others, his absolute involvement and absolute freedom, his penetrating truth and his triumphant acceptance of suffering and death, we see what man is meant to be. Through that death on the cross, man's alienation is overcome by the forgiveness of God and the way is opened for the restoration of all men to their sonship. In the resurrection of Jesus a new creation was born, and the final goal of history was assured, when Christ as head of that humanity will sum up all things.

On Christian/non-Christian dialogue, the report points out that it does not imply either a denial of the uniqueness of Christ or the weakening of commitment to Christ.

In dialogue we share our common humanity in dignity and fallenness, and express our common concern for that humanity. It opens the possibility of sharing in new forms of community and common service. Each meets and challenges the other, witnessing from the depths of his existence to the ultimate concern that comes to expression in word and action. As Christians we believe that Christ speaks in this dialogue, revealing himself to those who do not know him and correcting the limited and distorted knowledge of those who do.

The Uppsala report on the "The Holy Spirit and the Catholicity of the Church" clarified the relevance of the unity of the church to the search for the unity of humankind and emphasized the need for the churches to be open to "secular catholicities". It says:

The church is bold in speaking of itself as the sign of the coming unity of mankind. However well founded the claim, the world hears it sceptically, and points to "secular catholicities" of its own. For secular society has produced instruments of conciliation and unification which often seem more effective than the church itself... The churches need a new openness to the world in its aspirations, its achievements, its restlessness and its despair.

B. PAUL DEVANANDAN — THE HISTORICAL UNIVERSALITY OF THE NEW CREATION IN CHRIST

We have attempted a brief survey of the major trends in the theology of religions and secularism in the missionary/ecumenical movement of the last fifty years. It is only against the background of that history — receiving from it, criticizing it and going beyond it to make his own contribution to it — that we can understand the significance of Paul Devanandan's thought on interfaith relations in a pluralistic world.*

After his studies in the USA, Devanandan served as professor in history of religions at the United Theological College, Bangalore, for

*Devanandan never systematized his theology. In the course of five years as CISRS director (he died in 1962) his theology found expression in many articles and pamphlets. Perhaps Devanandan's address to the New Delhi Assembly of the World Council of Churches in 1961 comes nearest to spelling out the main elements of his theology of Christian witness in a pluralistic world. For the rest we have to go to his books *Gospel and Renascent Hinduism*, London, SCM, 1959; *The Dravida Kazhagam: a Revolt Against Brahminism*, Bangalore, CISRS, 1966; *The Concept of Maya: an Essay in Historical Survey of the Hindu Theory of the World with Special Reference to the Vedanta*, London, Lutterworth, 1950; *Christian Issues in South East Asia*, New York, (cont. on p. 86) many years. He was an ordained minister of the Church of South India. Later, he served as the secretary of the YMCA literature department for a period before he became the founder-director of the Christian Institute for the Study of Religion and Society (CISRS) sponsored by the National Christian Council in India. It was in this last capacity that he developed a programme of interfaith dialogue in the context of Christian participation in nation-building, and a Christological basis for such a dialogue, intergrating the renewal of "man-in-community" with our ultimate human destiny in Christ.

Devanandan first came under the influence of K.T. Paul's "Christian nationalism", the philosophy of religion from Berkeley and Yale Universities and Chenchiah's idea of Jesus as the new stage in the creative process. He was inclined towards the approach of Jerusalem 1928 which both K.T. Paul and P. Chenchiah supported. Then came Kraemer's *Christian Message in a Non-Christian World* and Tambaram 1938. Devanandan was influenced by Kraemer's Barthianism. But it also left him dissatisfied because of its negative attitude to the history of the search for religious truth and the struggle for human values in the national awakening. He began his search for an approach to the relation of Christianity to religious and secular history which went beyond Hocking and Kraemer and would incorporate the insights of K.T. Paul and P. Chenchiah about the Christian significance of participation in the national movement.

Christian witness — New Delhi 1961

We shall begin with Devanandan's address to the WCC Assembly in New Delhi, on the theme "Called to Witness".[53]

Here he speaks of the gospel to which the church is called to witness in three ways. First and foremost, it is "the reality of the New Creation in the Risen Christ as the one determining factor in world history which gives it significance and meaning, despite the confusion and disorder produced by man's endeavour to divert its destiny towards ends of his own devices".

Friendship Press, 1963; and more especially *Christian Concern in Hinduism*, with a foreword by S. Radhakrishnan, Bangalore, CISRS, 1961; and to collections of his essays, sermons and Bible studies published after his death: *Preparation for Dialogue*, eds Nalini Devanandan and M.M. Thomas, Bangalore, CISRS, 1964 and *I Will Lift up Mine Eyes*, eds S.J. Samartha and Nalini Devanandan, Bangalore, CISRS, 1963. Reference should also be made to the Devanandan memorial volume *Inter-religious Dialogue*, ed. Herbert Jai Singh, Bangalore, CISRS, 1967 and the doctoral thesis on his thought, *Theologie im Modernen Indien: Paul David Devanandan*, by Joachim Wietzke, Bern, Herbert Lang, 1975.

The New Creation in Christ is the true destiny of "the whole creation", for which all creation and all history have been longing and waiting (Rom. 8:19-24). Secondly, it is the message that "in Jesus Christ God is reconciling the world to himself" — bringing to human beings peace with God, the discovery of the wholeness of human personality. This work of redemption made manifest in human history in the life, death and resurrection of Jesus Christ is universal in scope; that is to say, it is "being carried out now and everywhere in our world; it is a present occurrence". Thirdly, it is the message that the kingdom is at hand, that Jesus as the incarnate word is "truly engaged in the world in the here and now that in the end, the end of time as man measures it and the end of history as man conceives of it, the whole creation will be transformed into a totally different realm of being where God's will is done". This is the substance of the hope that Jesus Christ will return to earth when he will "gather the whole world into his kingdom".

Thus the gospel is that God acted in Jesus to renew the whole creation and that that activity is continuing today in the Spirit of the Risen Jesus, re-creating humanity, and that in the end God will establish his kingdom on earth.

For Devanandan, however, the divine activity in Jesus for the world is from beginning to end a divine-human activity, and therefore an integral part of secular history, a new dimension in it which rules and over-rules it and leads it to its future. No doubt the faith-response on the part of human beings to the divine action is also God's work. "Only God himself can create the response of faith in men's hearts through the Holy Spirit." However, that faith-response is part of the cosmic and historical process which is renewed by it. As such it has fundamental this-worldly implications. Thus our evangelistic witness is "at the same time and for all times a cosmic process, a divine activity, a historical reality and a people's movement (which is) missionary in origin and intention and congregational in purpose and design".

It is in relation to this universal, cosmic, historical and people's movement for the renewal of all things that the church as the household of faith works "together with God, insofar as that is possible for man, in the task of extending the kingdom". Here the church becomes "the mission, the living outreach of God towards the world", "the earnest" of the New Creation in Christ. Devanandan emphasizes the historical corporate concreteness of the "local congregation" as representing "the community of the New Age in the context of the world-life in which it is placed". Only through the worship, the fellowship and service of the local churches can the saving power of God become manifest. The fellowship of the local congregation serves as the instrument of divine renewal. Where the local church becomes a "genuine and dynamic community" in Christ, it will spiritually penetrate its secular environment, and draw those outside into its koinonia.

Devanandan mentions three concrete "worlds" in which the church is to witness. First, the traditional village world. Here "the impact of the Christian koinonia on the group life of traditionally ordered society" mediates an awareness of the new quality of the life renewed in Christ. It is at this point that the village churches have witnessed or failed to witness to Christ.

Secondly, there is the modern secular world. Here Christian identity does not necessarily take visible religious form, but expresses itself in Christian solidarity with the secularity of the world. Christian witness is exercised in the world through identification with "the present concerns of secular life" in the farm, the factory and the market place. It is in terms of the everyday commerce of ordinary life of the lay world that the truth and meaning of Christ are communicated. This, says Devanandan, is in line with the principle of the incarnation: the word of God made flesh, the Son of God made like unto his brothers and sisters. The need that the church and its witness become "truly indigenous" is an extension of this principle. It is significant that the question of the church's indigenization is raised in the address first in its relation to the modern secular world. Indigenization of witness here means that

> together with their Lord, the *laos*, the people of God, must go forth to modern man where he is in his world of work, his family life, his leisure time, taking secular involvement seriously. There in his work-a-day world, we should learn to meet and talk together as men, as contemporary men, with the pressure of secularism upon us, with poverty for many a paramount and endless worry, with problems of choice to face daily, with a crying need to find some meaning in our existence.

However, Devanandan reminds us that this modern secular world has its corporate dimension of politics and technology which produces new problems and gives rise to new ideologies. The rise of Asian-African nationalism, the ideological struggle between democracy and communism coupled with the ever-increasing knowledge which now extends to outer space, have all created new "dramatic transformations" in the socio-political patterns of life. He specially mentions that there is a deep suspicion of the white races in many parts of the world because of their racist attitudes. In such a world the church of Christ "must address itself to the concrete realities of the contemporary situation in order to express more fully in human relations God's will for peace, justice, equality and freedom on earth". Here a genuine human community manifesting the koinonia in Christ is the goal of Christian witness. Devanandan adds that the church can work for a global human community only if it recognizes the pluralistic character of the world and is "willing to cross all frontiers in their relations with one another" in the name of Christ. Evidently, he has in mind all the frontiers between Christianity and the non-Christian religions and secularist ideologies.

Thirdly, the "world of other faiths". Here we are not dealing with just the other religions, but with "the surging new life manifest in other religions especially in Asian lands". Traditional Christian approaches, which think of different religions as staying within "traditionally accepted boundaries of beliefs and practices", are not adequate to interpret the modern renaissance of other religions. Nor are the sociological and psychological explanations. Devanandan affirms that "if religious faith is to be regarded also in terms of response it would be difficult for the Christian to deny that these deep inner stirrings of the human spirit are in response to the creative activity of the Holy Spirit". The only alternative is to confess either the Christian ignorance of God's ways with people or the Christian blindness in refusing to believe in God's redemptive work with people of other faiths.

In any case, says Devanandan, the claim of the living non-Christian religions on the emerging world community cannot be denied or evaded. "The living faith of contemporary non-Christian religions makes a bold bid in our generation to give form and content not only to the distinctive patterns of our national cultures, but also to the total fabric of world-culture." And Christian ecumenism has to reckon with this demand.

The imperatives of religious pluralism in the modern world are not merely at the cultural level. We have a situation in which the "values" of culture and community interpenetrate inevitably with "ultimate" truths and goals. No doubt there is a breakdown of communication in depth in our secularized world. But in another sense, the modern world with its demand for global community on a pluralistic basis has opened up new possibilities of participating in life and in dialogue on life at depth across traditional frontiers of faith.

> We may not forget that among men of faith who are adherents of renascent religions as well as those who profess no faith at all, there exists a common

> universe of discourse based on spontaneous reactions to the totality of life. We are all involved in a common crisis, tied together by a community of interests; our common humanity serves as a common denominator; and on the frontiers of renascent faiths, doctrinal barriers no longer foreclose religious commerce.

Devanandan further notes that the renaissance of non-Christian religions has in many ways come about as a result of the impact on them of Christianity or Christian aspects of modern secularism, and that therefore "many Christian truths", divorced from their original context and reinterpreted and reformulated in traditional categories of other religions, may be found in them. Also, their own traditional religious truths are reinterpreted and reformulated in more or less Christian or secular terms to meet the demands of our time. All this shows that there has been "increasing traffic across the border". Inter-religious encounters have produced intra-religious dialogues at depth. This situation calls for "no mere study of the scriptural foundations of the historical religions in their classical expression" but a sympathetic understanding of them as living contemporary religions.

Such intra-dialogue leading to the renaissance of other religions needs to be met by an equally deep intra-faith dialogue within Christianity. There is need to assimilate non-Christian religious truths by reinterpreting and reformulating them in the light of Christ and also to express Christian truths in non-Christian religious categories. Here Devanandan expresses a basic theological principle:

> If God's redemptive activity in Jesus Christ is a fact with which we should reckon in every human situation, it is not so much by total destruction that he manifests his power but by radical renewal of what we cherish as valuable. That is why the gospel we proclaim is the good news of the resurrection, the hope of the New Creation.

In this light can we go on saying that the gospel is directed at the total annihilation of all religions other than Christianity? Or is there a place for other religions renewed in Christ in the history of God's kingdom on earth? And what about the ultimate End? "Will religions as religions and nations as nations continue characteristically separate in the fullness of times when God would gather together in one all things in Christ, things which are in heaven and things which are on earth?" Devanandan answers that it is not for us to indicate what will be preserved and in what manner; we are now called only to "identify ourselves with the will of God as revealed in Christ" and wait for the "final gathering up of this world and of the next in the resurrection-life".

Devanandan distinguishes between the ideas of fulfilment held by the historian of religion and the theologian of religion. The historian discerns a more or less historical progression in the human understanding of God from the primitive religious past, through the living present, to what will be perfected in the future. There may well be a fulfilment of that kind. However the gospel proclamation is about the fulfilment of the promise of the kingdom. Here it is not the past evolving into the present and naturally fulfilled in the future. Rather, it is the ultimate future being fulfilled in the present:

> Because the promise of the kingdom is so totally assured, the end in reality is a present fact. It is come! In salvation history, to the discerning eye of faith the eternal future is being fulfilled in the contemporary present. It is in this sense that our Lord declared that he has come not to destroy but to fulfill.
>
> This is the scandal in the foolishness of Christian witness to the historical and particular, to Jesus Christ as revealing the timeless and eternal God.

Let us take up some of the theological themes touched on in Devanandan's New Delhi address, in order to gain an understanding of his theology of religions and secular ideological pluralism and to expand it in the light of his other writings.

The gospel of New Creation in Jesus

Throughout Devanandan's writings the gospel is presented as the good news of new creation in Jesus Christ. "The good news we proclaim, following the way of the apostles, is the good news of this new creation. That was the burden of the Apostles' preaching, and that is still the Christian message." Devanandan spells out some of its characteristics.

First, the new creation in Jesus Christ has personal, social and cosmic dimensions. "If any man be in Christ he is a new creation" — the renewal of person. It also means the birth of a new humanity. "With the coming of Jesus Christ a new humanity is not only in the making, it has been brought into being." It means also the recreation of the whole cosmos. "Biblical faith repeatedly affirms that the work of Christ is of cosmic significance in that the redemption wrought in him has affected the entire creative process" (Col. 1:16-20). This total transformation of all things is the essence of the peace, wholeness and reconciliation Christ has brought. If at the threshold of this century the church became aware of a social gospel besides the personal one, "perhaps as we reach the middle of this century", says Devanandan, "we are coming to realize that the total sweep of the Good News envelops God's entire creation. The ultimate end is a new heaven and a new earth, a new creation. How utterly impossible can it be for any fragment of mankind to be changed or even for all humanity to be transformed, unless the grossly material and purely animal content of world-life is also transformed? Is that not why the fact of the Risen Lord forms the core of the Gospel we proclaim?"[54]

Secondly, the new creation in Christ means newness in the present. No doubt, it is an eschatological reality to be manifested in its completeness in the second coming of Christ, but it is also the future made real in the present. It is the reality of new creation in the "present now" which is crucial. Devanandan therefore speaks of the risen Christ as the "contemporary Christ". The renewing power of the new creation is available for "people living in the storm and stress of all the complexities of the world of rapid changes". "The present reality of the creative work of God, even in all the perplexing confusion of contemporary events, distinguishes the Christian faith from other faiths. This fact is what we proclaim in the person and work of our Lord Jesus Christ."[55]

Nevertheless, the power of new creation in the present is not just a miracle of the moment. As the realization of the future in the present, it directs the present to the future, and also has a continuity in history directing human history to its divine end. That is, the new creation is also a creative process within the cosmic and historical processes, transforming them and giving them a new dynamic, meaning and direction here and now. The continuity of the new creation in human history, however, is not the continuity of a "self-contained process" but of a "continuous act" of divine grace. It is not something that touches human history from without as a tangent touches a circle, but it becomes a process taking hold of the march of human history from within, giving it shape and direction. And it makes it possible for faith to look for the signs of God's new creation in Christ not only in the transformed lives of individuals but also in the struggles of peoples to renew structures of society, culture and religion.

Devanandan's theology of history is related to this. He says:

> What we call a particular circumstance in history is constituted in the main of three elements. It is the outcome of the impersonal working of nature's laws; added to it are the factors created by human decisions; but beneath it all, ruling and over-ruling the ongoing process of history, is the redemptive will of God. There is an abiding value in every passing human condition that is God's secret. It is secret because it concerns his ultimate design. And yet, at any moment in history, though many things happen, what is of real and lasting value is this secret intention of God that is shaping the entire process of history

> towards the final end which God has in view. God was in Christ reconciling the world unto himself. The dynamic presence of the supernatural is cleansing, healing, redeeming at all points in human history. Only in releasing that presence does man's life at any time gain meaning and significance.[56]

Thirdly, the scandal of particularity is the essence of the universality of the new creation. The new creation is mediated through the unique revelatory act of God in the person and work of Jesus in his life, death and resurrection and the resurrection-life bestowed in the Holy Spirit.

In his address to a conference of the Fellowship of the Friends of Truth in Gandhigram, India, on "The Exclusive Claims of Christianity", Devanandan sought to relate uniqueness to universality:

> Christian faith is that what God has done in Jesus Christ has been done for all men. So that the claim of uniqueness is only an affirmation of its universality... Christians believe that with the coming of Christ, God Almighty identified himself for a while with man in all man's struggles for perfection and the realization of his true nature. Such identification initiates a new era in creation. It marks the beginning of a redemptive movement which takes in humanity in its entirety, that is the whole community of mankind, inclusive of all peoples, whatever their beliefs, language or race.[57]

It is not only that the "redemptive purpose in the incarnation is all-inclusive", but also that "the whole creation in all its being is already redeemed by the work of Christ, that the gospel is primarily the good news of this new order of being, calling men to accept what they already are".[58] This places all humanity in the position of having to recognize the reality of an "objective redemption" or refusing to recognize it. And further, the recognition of this universal reality could take many forms, not necessarily the Christian religious form. It also means that any easy distinction between the believer and the unbeliever should be avoided, especially since the traffic across the borders has become heavy.[59]

This raises the question of the relation of the church to the new creation. The church, as the fellowship of those acknowledging and witnessing to the Lordship of Jesus Christ, is for Devanandan an integral ingredient in God's design for the world's redemption. The "invitation to join the church" is extended by Jesus Christ himself. However, Devanandan disclaims the idea of the church as "an exclusive community that claims for itself a special privilege with God". It would not be true to say either that "there is no salvation outside the church" or that there is salvation for all who are inside. The church is not a closed body, but an open one emphasizing discipleship to Jesus. Faith, even extraordinary faith, is to be found outside the church, because the Spirit is universally at work. Indeed, says Devanandan, "the church is not only built by the Spirit of God working within it but also by the Spirit of God working outside it. In either case it is the work of God for the transformation of those who endeavour to do his will."[60] That is why the church is engaged in a double movement — the centrifugal one of drawing people into the church and the centripetal one of the church reaching out into the world outside. "This should save us from the danger of confusing the mere expansion of the church with the extension of the kingdom. And yet it is difficult to see how the realm of God's sovereignty can be extended unless there come into being more and more people who commit themselves to the Lordship of Christ."[61]

Fourthly, Devanandan's concept of God and revelation does not make the redemptive process in history either totally hidden or totally understandable to faith. It is a reality which faith is able to discern in every human situation, to the extent necessary for human participation in the renewing activity of the Spirit in that situation.

Devanandan accepts the concept of God as the wholly Other, but with radical qualifications.

> God is wholly other, in every way different from the nature of things we men are used to. The realm of God's true being is on another plane than what we call the natural. Seeking to know God from the behaviour of the universe tends to identify God with the substance of this every-day world.
>
> We need to remind ourselves that God and world experiences are essentially contradictory. He is other-than-the-world, other-than-I. That is why at the heart of all theology there will always be an element of unfathomable mystery.[62]

But Devanandan also asserts that God cannot just be wholly other. "He cannot be satisfied with being the wholly other, the Unknowable Unknown from everlasting to everlasting, the eternal Brahman. Not the Father of our Lord Jesus Christ." Therefore, the mystery of God's ways are "not hidden from the insight of those to whom God chooses to reveal them, that seeing they may perceive and hearing they may understand". So, while there is faith that trusts and rests assured, there is also the understanding that expects God to let us into God's secrets, "that we may work with and for Him". Thus not only the ultimate end but also the pattern of God's action for judgment and redemption in contemporary situations is in some measure revealed to faith. This discerning of the times is the basis of prophecy and service.

Interpretation of the modern religious situation

Within the framework of a theology of new creation which relates the unique revelation of God in the crucified and risen Jesus Christ to the universality of the historical movement of divine grace renewing persons, cultures and the cosmos, Devanandan develops his theology of religion and religious pluralism in the modern world.

Here Devanandan's starting point is that of Dialectical Theology — that the revelation in Jesus Christ which justifies humanity by grace through faith exposes religion as sinful humanity's search for self-justification through idolatry and abolishes it. From this starting point we have already seen Barth and Kraemer moving in the direction of revelation justifying and sanctifying Christianity as "true religion", as the means of grace; and Bonhoeffer and van Leeuwen justifying by faith a religionless or secular Christianity. Devanandan seems to take a third path which explores the possibility of revelation judging, justifying and renewing other religions also so as to make them true religious partners with justified Christianity and justified secularism in witnessing to and participating in the recreation of the modern world in Christ.

The central emphasis in Devanandan's theology of religion is on the meaning of the cross as exposing all search for justification by the works of the law, including religion, as enmity to God. The cross also reveals free divine forgiveness which breaks the hold of law, breaks down all middle walls of partition between people set up by law (religion) and unites them in the new plane of being in Christ's new humanity. It also sends them back into their religions to critique and renew them in the light of their common humanity renewed in Christ. The cross of Jesus Christ is thus the vision of a common humanity transcending religions and secular quasi-religions, and of a power to break down their rigid boundary walls and to participate with each other in witnessing to the new humanity in Christ.

Devanandan's thought here is related to his exegesis of Ephesians 2:14-16:

> For he is our peace, who has made us both one, and has broken down the dividing wall of hostility by abolishing in his flesh the law of commandments and ordinances, that he might create in himself one new man in place of the two, so making peace, and might reconcile us both to God in one body through the cross, thereby bringing the hostility to an end.

Devanandan sees here the cross ending the Jew-Gentile religious hostility by abolishing the law (religion) which created the division, and by bringing about free justification by faith. And he raises the possibility of an extension of this to the religious divisions of our time.

Of course, the order of new being in Christ will co-exist with the old order of religion till it is consummated in the End. But even in this stage of co-existence of the two orders, the cross provides a permanent critique of religion and the power to renew it constantly towards converting it into the true religion mediating grace. This is so not only for Christianity as Barth and Kraemer maintain. So long as it is the divine grace in Christ alone that justifies and transforms idolatrous Christianity into true religion, such renewal can happen to any religion or secularism, provided it opens itself to the ferment of the cross of Christ within it. It also means that where people are drawn to the divine humanity of Jesus revealed on the cross, we should expect the religious walls that separate them to break down, making possible a new community of dialogue. And Devanandan shows not only that these things can happen but also that this is the direction in which things do happen in the present renaissance of non-Christian religions and secular quasi-religions.

> The word of the cross needs to be preached today in the conviction that because Christ rose again, what man calls religion — the reign of law — is of the earth, earthy, of the old things to pass away. This is a daring thought; and it may well be fraught with dangerous heresy. But Christians of this generation may give heed to it. As we enter a new era in world history, we need to question ourselves whether we witness to a gospel that perpetuates this very enmity which God in Christ has destroyed, or do we proclaim the word of reconciliation?[63]

Does this not necessitate absolutizing the distinction between Christianity and other religions as Kraemer does? Devanandan's answer is, it need not. The concentric circles of creed, cultus and culture all together comprise the total area of outreach and influence of any religion. The faith of a religion is expressed in and through these circles and hence they are tied to the faith. But they are not identical with the faith itself and should not be absolutized. Faith transcends religion. This is true for Christianity as for other religions. Faith in Christ transcends the Christian religion. As Devanandan puts it: "All religions are historical phenomena and Christianity is no exception. As any other religion, it has also been subject to the process of change in human history. Its organizational structure, its interpretation of the fundamentals of the Christian faith, have all been subject to limitations of the human mind and of human effort. But it is not Christianity that is preached as against other religions.

The message of the Christian witness is the gospel around which Christianity as a historical phenomenon has developed."[64]

Therefore, our message is the person of Jesus crucified, understood as the divine re-creation of humanity. Insofar as other religions have been grappling with Jesus and his cross and his humanity "any easy distinction which we set up between the believer and the unbeliever" based on Christian religious doctrine often breaks down. "True, we may not minimize the doctrine. But the insidious danger is in forgetting that doctrines are also, in a sense, symbolic. They stand for a reality which they do not always fully represent nor totally exhaust. Therefore to reduce the distinction between a believer and an unbeliever by the rigid pattern of a creed or the externals of a ritual act is to fall into the same error which persisted in distinguishing Jew from Gentile in the early church."[65]

Faith is seen at the level of self-commitment. If Christian faith is the acknowledgment of Christ's Lordship in human self-commitment, one meets it among the adherents of non-Christian religions as well in their renascent phase. Here Devanandan does not mean that the distinction between belief and unbelief is at the level of ethics. In fact, in discussing "Gandhi's critique of Christianity" Devanandan criticizes Gandhi for reducing the meaning of the cross to the ethical principle of absolute love. He says that the affirmation of Christian faith is not that there is an ethical standard of goodness to be achieved by the human person in order to qualify for the gift of God's grace, but rather that the ethic of love is "made possible for mankind only when they have been totally transfigured by the new creation in Christ". He adds: "No Christian would deny that God did give Gandhiji his enabling grace to live the sermon on the Mount to the extent that he did as a *satyagrahi*. For to that extent, Gandhiji acknowledged Jesus Christ as Lord and sought to do the will of God in his life for his time."[66] Here Devanandan sees the partial acknowledgment of Christ in Gandhi, not in his doctrinal and ethical interpretations of Jesus but in his grappling with and his positive life-response to the person of Jesus and his new humanity, though this is done from within his own religion of Hinduism.

This raises the question of Devanandan's theological interpretation of the resurgence and restatement of all religions. That is an ongoing process caused partly by the meeting of living faiths on the plane of religion and culture and partly because of the struggle in all religions and cultures for fuller human life through a greater mastery of nature, a recognition of the fundamental dignity of human persons and deeper interpersonal relations in social institutions, and through the development of world community. Rapid changes are taking place in the beliefs, religious practices and cultures of peoples. But what do they imply for the self-understanding, self-transcendence and self-commitment at the core of religious faiths? Does the resurgence of the ancient religions of Asia and their restatement today under the impact of Christianity and secular humanism informed by the gospel of Christ indicate an activity of Christ to destroy "the middle wall of partition" between religions so as to prepare them for the new humanity in Christ which transcends all religions?

Devanandan's answers to these questions are tentative but they indicate a positive note. Speaking again on Christ's work reconciling the Jew and the Gentile, Devanandan asks: "Does that mean that with Christ the neat boundaries of the religions of mankind have been broken down? In what we call the resurgence of faith in the non-Christian world, perhaps we do not sufficiently reckon with the new state of affairs where the traffic across the borders has become heavy." He goes on to show that in this new state of affairs created by the resurgence of non-Christian religions, there are signs of new decisions of faith in relation to Christ, both of positive response and militant rejection.

> How much of what is called restatement of non-Christian beliefs and practices is restatement to make them relevant to modern life? How much of it is restatement in fact in the light of non-Christian understanding of the gospel? Why is it that modern Hindu leaders, for instance, do not restate their beliefs in terms of modern Buddhism or Islam, but in terms of what they think is the Christian gospel? Is the modern man's rejection of Christ — at any rate in Asia — because Christianity is an alien religion which stands for a foreign culture? Or is it because he finds that in a very real sense the middle wall of partition is breaking down and he wants to put it up again? We may not expect men of non-Christian renascent faiths to openly acknowledge that the ferment in their religious thinking and the new emphasis they place on values which we regard as distinctively Christian are both due to the influence of the gospel. But to those who see human history with the eye of faith, it is apparent that the fact of Christ has made an obvious difference, and that it continues to make a difference in the living and thinking of men of all faiths. He has made both one, and has broken down the wall of partition.[67]

Elsewhere Devanandan gives a description of renascent Hinduism engaged in the task of integrating the values of Western science and humanism on its own theological foundations, and concludes: "One cannot resist the impulse of faith that believes in a God who is also the

Lord of history, and in a creative Spirit who is ever at work in the world of men, redeeming it even in its present involvements and directing its course to the ultimate fulfilment of his purpose, that in all religious revival God is somehow at work."[68] He sees this as a challenge to the church to discern that work of God and relate itself to it.

Devanandan repeats this interpretation of the Asian renaissance and revolution in another form. He says that "if the whole creation is being directed by the redemptive act of God in Jesus Christ towards the final hope of glory" and "if the true reading of salvation-history is in terms of Eternity flowing into Time", the task of the church is to see how the ultimate future is being fulfilled or realized in the temporal present — and therefore also in the present renaissance of life in Asia. The church thus is called upon to "restate the distinctiveness of the gospel in the context of the religions of the world" with a sense of the "real significance of the newness in contemporary Hinduism, Buddhism and Islam" through which the Spirit of God is guiding peoples to "a new understanding of God's ways with the world of men today".[69]

Where does Devanandan discern the renewing and creative work of the Spirit of Christ in the renaissance of ancient religions? He sees it primarily in their awakening to the new dimensions of human existence, namely personality, personal community and purposive history. These dimensions, in his opinion, have a direct or indirect relation to the biblical faith in the God of history who, as the Father of our Lord Jesus Christ, is actively creating and recreating a human community patterned after the cruciform humanity of Jesus. Therefore, Devanandan discerns Christ's activity in other religions, not in their classical theology and spirituality but in their struggle to assimilate the new anthropology into the traditional theological and spiritual framework and to give it the support of a reinterpreted tradition.

Even in his earlier writings Devanandan was concerned with this phenomenon in relation to Hinduism. He wrote:

> The determinative doctrine in the evaluation of the Hindu outlook on life is no longer derived from its classical theology, but is built upon a new anthropology. This anthropology is perhaps still in the making. Nevertheless the primary question that is of dominant concern to the modern Hindu thinker is the nature and destiny of man — what is man and whither is he bound.[70]

In his *Concept of Maya* Devanandan studies the manner in which the traditional Hindu concept of the world, *maya*, is being reinterpreted to provide a basis for the historical humanism associated with Indian nationalism, and the tension experienced in the heart of Hinduism between the classical view of life and the new way of life. The question, as he sees it in the conclusion of the study, is "whether it will be possible for Hinduism out of itself, unaided, to produce from its founts of religious theory an articulate, reasoned system, an adequate creed as a basis of belief, which will provide the needed intellectual justification and spiritual drive for this new Hindu way of life". He also makes the point that in seeking to answer this question, thoughtful Indians are realizing the "inadequacy of the Upanishadic assumptions", and the need for their "complete transformation" if Hinduism is to furnish the living inspiration and the theological theory to the remodelling of Hindu society on the basis of true personal values. It is this realization that makes the present "a time of renaissance, a rebirth, the coming into being of a new creation, the dynamic rejuvenation of Hinduism".[71]

Later Devanandan surveys the whole history of the modern movements of Indian renaissance from the Brahma Samaj, the Arya Samaj and the Ramakrishna Mission of the nineteenth century, through Gandhian Sarvodaya and the philosophies of Aurobindo and Radhakrishnan and the anti-Brahminism of E.V. Ramaswamy Naicker and B.R. Ambedkar, to the Hindu secularism of Jawaharlal Nehru and Jayaprakash Narain. He shows how running through it all is an attempt to examine the relation between classical Hindu tradition and the new imperative for a dynamic social humanism. In the more religious of these movements there is a persistent effort to reinterpret the metaphysical and mystical tradition in order to reconcile it with the new historical secular imperatives. And even the secularistically oriented movements attempt to define the meaning of true religion.[72]

Devanandan deals with the creative aspect of Neo-Vedantic efforts to provide the spiritual foundation for new India:

> The more recent trend is to turn to the *Bhagavad Gita* for scriptural authority. Hindu religious leaders expound the basic teachings of the *Gita* more in terms of a theistic interpretation of the Brahman than in terms of a rigorous monism... Even so, the stumbling block continues to be the supreme difficulty of putting meaning-content into the term "personal" as applied to God and his relationship with man, especially in view of the "new" significance given in contemporary Hindu society to the concept of the human "person" in relation to other persons. The other difficulty arises when the point is made that beyond all the activism, openly admitted as theologically valid, there is the "actionlessness" of mystic *advaitum* (non-duality) of the finite self and the infinite self still upheld as the one desirable end of all religious pilgrimage. Even in its theistic form the Vedanta is not able to overcome this

> problem of reconciling the active life of the temporal here and now with the mystic quietude of the eternal present.[73]

Hinduism has its peculiar problem of relating its "classical theology" to the "new anthropology". So have all the other religions, including Christianity and secular quasi-religions. What Devanandan wishes to affirm is that in the new concern for "person", "history" and "community", all faiths are brought into the same circle of theological-anthropological concerns and into the orbit of the process of a common history; and further, that in creating this common situation of contemporary history the gospel of the New Humanity in Jesus Christ plays a part. For these reasons, all faiths are compelled to open themselves (or close themselves more firmly) to one another and to Jesus Christ in a new way.

Christian ecumenism

It is this context of contemporary history and the crisis it brings to all religions, ideologies and cultures that calls for a Christianity which discerns the signs of the times and responds to Christ in an ecumenical witness. What are some of the chief characteristics of this witness?

First it calls for a change of emphasis in Christian thought concerning evangelism — from Jesus Christ as the revelation of God to Jesus Christ as the revelation of the new creation of God in human history, from mere theocentricism to theocentric humanism meeting the human quest for all humanity. Devanandan sees "Christian participation in nation-building" in forming, together with others, new patterns of human community on a pluralistic basis, and the interfaith dialogue on the meaning of being human within that framework, as not merely service, but service with an interpretation of the gospel of Christ integrated in it.

Devanandan's main contribution to Christian ecumenism lies in his stimulation of interfaith dialogue as an ongoing concern of the church in the common search for human community. Here the emphases are on "our common humanity" and "a secular framework" within which people of all religions and no religion can work together to enrich the common life. The secular framework requires the recognition of religious freedom as a fundamental right of the human person, and of religious plurality in the body-politic. At the same time it challenges all people to the twofold task of "redeeming all religions from the other-worldly preoccupation of pietism on the one hand and self-centred introversion of communalism on the other". Here, secularism itself is an ally. Devanandan says that the task of the Christian evangelist is "not so much to counter forces of secularism and irreligion" but to help people in city and village, at all levels of culture, to "redefine the very nature of what is called religion". All faiths must clarify their respective views on the common humanity and the secularity which expresses it and of the place and function of religion and religions in the process of building a common culture. To this conversation Christians must bring their gospel of the common life, of the possibility of deliverance from the bondage to forms of evil that are of human creation.

To be sure, says Devanandan, it is the Father's good pleasure to give us the kingdom. But it is no less true that the earnest of that gift in the conditions of the here and now implies our joining forces with those of other faiths in "waging war against all poverty, diseases and oppression of all sorts". In such an endeavour we are witnessing to the new creation in Christ, "within this sin-bound world of sin, conscious of ourselves as also still tainted by the solidarity of human sinfulness in which we too share."[74] Thus the Christian basis of common humanity is human solidarity in sin and in the grace of Jesus Christ and his kingdom which is both here and hereafter. It is this that we contribute to the dialogue, not in the abstract but as together we seek to define the goals and means of a common human society and culture, and work together to achieve it.

In the partnership in social action "the concern is human *welfare* as an immediate goal with no reference to the ultimate destiny of man". But it does not mean that human welfare has no relation to the ultimate human destiny. Here, says Devanandan, there is need for mutual understanding among the partners at spiritual depth, which can come only through dialogue about the foundations of human dignity and welfare in each other's faith.

The dialogue referred to here is not only of the formal kind, but more significant are the informal dialogues which become normal among persons of different religious persuasions in the context of daily life and work. It is carried on within a community of mutual confidence in each other's personal integrity in the face of ultimate Truth. Says Devanandan: "We need to know much more than we do now of the living faiths of other men, and even more of the faith whereby we ourselves live."

Secondly, there is a Christian concern in the reinterpretation taking place in the classical traditions of other religions. There is also the possibility of the church's participating sensitively in their renaissance. Nalini Devadas has traced the evolution of Devanandan's concern with Neo-Hindu interpretations of the Hindu traditions from within, from his earlier book *The Concept of Maya* to the later *Christian Concern in Hinduism*, in this light. In the latter, she finds the idea of a "deliberate self-emptying by which a Christian is willing to stay with the Hindu in this task of reinterpretation — to think Hinduism with the Hindu".[75] The idea of "the deliberate self-emptying of Christianity in other religions", the seed of which Nalini Devadas sees in Devanandan's thought, has great potentialities of development for the future of Christianity in the world of religions.

Thirdly, Devanandan follows Hocking in advocating a "process of reconception" of every historical religion in the light of other religions. That is, the goal of inter-religious and intra-religious dialogues is here defined as a common culture or civilization with a plurality of religions each redefining itself in the light of the others and assimilating truths and values from others on its own faith-core. Devanandan explains it as follows: "By process of reconception, every religion should reconceive its own essence so as somehow to include as a new element in its own essence the essence of other religions. In this way, we do not commit ourselves to an enduring plurality of religions or to an amalgamation of religions."[76]

It is not clear what the word "essence" here means. But considering his total approach, one may presume that he has in mind the following elements: (1) A movement towards a composite culture inspired by a common humanity with openness towards different faiths and their contributions to the common pool. The worldwide process of secularization, technological advance and social revolution is dissolving religious cultures; and cultural reintegration has to be in the direction of a common national or even world culture, no doubt with local variations. (2) A more radical reinterpretation at the level of religious creed and cultus of each religion absorbing elements from other religions and integrating them in the fundamental core of its faith and within the context of the struggle for a common culture. This will mean bringing into Christianity as much as possible of the symbolism of indigenous religions, not in their traditional forms but radically changed to be the vehicle of the Christian faith and to be consistent with the ecumenism of world Christianity and the humanism of the emerging world culture. (3) A meeting of different religions at the core of their faiths, whether through propagation or dialogue, leading to greater mutual understanding, and openness even to conversion. It is quite possible, says Devanandan, "that when a man has experienced the fact of genuine religious conversion, he may feel impelled to move out from one fellowship to another, because of an inner constraint that the new commitment involves such a step". According to Devanandan it is possible to develop a common language of theological discourse between two religions, though not a common theology.

NOTES

[1] Quoted by Carl Hallencreutz, *Kraemer Towards Tambaram*, Lund, Gleerup, 1966, pp.196-197.
[2] By the Commission of Appraisal, William Ernest Hocking, Chairman, New York, 1932.
[3] *Living Religions and a World Faith*, London, Allen & Unwin, 1940, p.26.
[4] *Ibid.*, p.198.
[5] *The Coming World Civilisation*, New York, Harper, 1956, p.136.
[6] *Living Religions, op. cit.*, p.269.
[7] *Ibid.*, p.169.
[8] *The Coming World Civilisation, op. cit.*, p.113.
[9] *Living Religions, op. cit.*, p.235.
[10] *Ibid.*, p.145.
[11] Second quarter, 1932.
[12] Quoted by Nicol Macnicol, *Is Christianity Unique*, London, SCM Press, 1936, pp.168-171.
[13] *The Epistle to the Romans*, translated from the sixth edition by Edwyn C. Hoskyns, new preface by the author, London, Oxford University Press, 1933, p.236.
[14] *Ibid.*, p.253.
[15] *Ibid.*, p.331.
[16] Vol. I, "The Doctrine of the Word of God", para. 2, section 17. "The Revelation of God as the Abolition of Religion", Edinburgh, T.& T.Clark, 1963, pp.280-361.
[17] *Christian Faith in a Religiously Pluralistic World*, eds Donald Dawe and John Carman, New York, Orbis, 1978, pp.90-92.
[18] *The Christian Message in a Non-Christian World*, New York, Harper, 1938, p.125.
[19] *Ibid.*, p.113.
[20] Philadelphia, Westminster Press, 1956, p.193.
[21] London, Lutterworth, 1962.
[22] *Christian Message, op. cit.*, p.146.
[23] *Why Christianity of All Religions, op. cit.*, p.109.
[24] *Ibid.*, p.114.
[25] *Ibid.*, p.119.
[26] "Dietrich Bonhoeffer and Karl Barth's Positivism of Revelation", by R. Prenter, in *World Come of Age*, ed. Ronald G. Smith, Philadelphia, Fortress Press, 1967, pp.106-121.
[27] With special reference to Hendrik Kraemer and Alfred George Hogg as well as to William Ernest Hocking and Pandipeddi Chenchiah, Berne, Las Vegas, P. Lang, 1981.
[28] *Karma and Redemption: an Essay Toward the Interpretation of Hinduism and the Restatement of Christianity*, London, Madras, Colombo, 1909; *Christ's Message of the Kingdom*, Edinburgh, 1911; *Redemption from this World*, Edinburgh, T.& T.Clark, 1922; *Christian Message to the Hindu*, London, SCM Press, 1947.
[29] *International Review of Missions*, 1914, p.173.
[30] In Eric Sharpe ed., *Theology of Hogg*, Madras, CISRS/CLS, 1971, pp.206-222.
[31] *Religious Truth and the Relation Between Religions*, Madras, CLS, 1950, pp.143-159.
[32] Eds D.M. Devaschayam and A.N. Sudarisanam, "A Review of Dr Kraemer's Book" by P. Chenchiach, Appendix, 1-54.
[33] D.A. Thangasamy, *Theology of Chenchiah* (with selections from his writings), Bangalore, CISRS/CLS, 1966, p.177.

[34] *Rethinking, op. cit.*, appendix, p.17.
[35] *Ibid.*, p.27.
[36] *Ibid.*, p.24.
[37] *Ibid.*, p.43.
[38] *Theology of Chenchiah, op. cit.*, p.216.
[39] *Christian Faith in a Religiously Pluralistic World, op. cit.*, p.90.
[40] *World Come of Age, op. cit.*, p.95.
[41] *Letters and Papers from Prison*, enlarged ed., ed. E. Bethge, London, SCM, 1971, p.282.
[42] Translated by B. Noble, New York, Harper, 1961.
[43] Ed. E. Bethge, translated by H. Smith, New York, Macmillan, 1955.
[44] *Letters and Papers from Prison, op. cit.*, pp.280-281.
[45] Foreword by H. Kraemer, London, Edinburgh House, 1964.
[46] Stanley Samartha, "Mission and Movements of Innovation", *Third World Theologies,* (Mission Trends No. 3), eds A. Anderson and T. Stransky, New York, Paulist, 1976, pp.234,237.
[47] In *Christian Prospect in Eastern Asia*, East Asia Christian Conference, Bangkok 1949, New York, Friendship Press, 1950.
[48] *The Christian Community within the Human Community*, an EACC document, Bangalore, 1964, pp.17-35.
[49] *Church's Witness* (in relation to religion and society, international affairs, religious liberty — programme for 1964-8), Madras, EACC, 1964, pp.30-34.
[50] Douglas J. Elword ed, *Asian Christian Theology — Emerging Themes*, revised ed. of *What Asians are Thinking*, Philadelphia, Westminster Press, 1980, pp.43-47.
[51] *Ibid.*, p.45.
[52] *Uppsala 1968*, ed. Norman Goodall, Geneva, WCC, pp.27-36.
[53] *Preparation for Dialogue: Essays on Hinduism and Christianity in New India*, eds Nalini Devanandan and M.M. Thomas, Bangalore, CISRS, 1964, pp.179-193.
[54] *Christian Concern in Hinduism*, foreword by S. Radhakrishnan, Bangalore, CISRS, 1961, pp.118-120.
[55] *I Will Lift Up Mine Eyes to the Hills: Sermons and Bible Studies of Paul D. Devanandan*, eds S.J. Samartha and Nalini Devanandan, Bangalore, CISRS, 1963, p.67.
[56] *Ibid.*, pp.21-22.
[57] *Preparation for Dialogue, op. cit.*, pp.137-138.
[58] *Christian Concern in Hinduism, op. cit.*, p.108.
[59] *I Will Lift Up Mine Eyes, op. cit.*, p.118.
[60] *Preparation for Dialogue, op. cit.*, p.117.
[61] *Ibid.*, p.117.
[62] *I Will Lift Up Mine Eyes, op. cit.*, pp.15-16.
[63] *Ibid.*, p.126.
[64] *Preparation for Dialogue, op. cit.*, p.114.
[65] *I Will Lift Up Mine Eyes, op. cit.*, pp.114-115.
[66] *Preparation for Dialogue, op. cit.*, p.111.
[67] *I Will Lift Up Mine Eyes, op. cit.*, p.118.
[68] *Christian Concern in Hinduism, op. cit.*, p.82.
[69] *Preparation for Dialogue, op. cit.*, p.177.
[70] *Christian Concern in Hinduism, op. cit.*, p.112.
[71] Quoted from Nalini Devadas in *Inter-religious Dialogue*, ed. Herbert Jai Singh, Bangalore, CISRS, 1967, pp.24-25, footnote.
[72] *Preparation for Dialogue, op. cit.*, pp.1-79.
[73] *Ibid.*, pp.10-11.
[74] *Christian Concern in Hinduism, op. cit.*, p.ix-x.
[75] *Inter-religious Dialogue, op. cit.*, p.24-26.
[76] *Preparation for Dialogue*, p.144.

4. Issues in the Debate: a Concluding Comment

We have surveyed the major ecumenical trends in the theology of religious and ideological pluralism and studied in some detail the thought of Raymond Panikkar and Paul Devanandan against their Catholic and Protestant theological backgrounds.

Let us briefly look at some of the criticisms levelled against the understanding of Christ and the church explicit or implicit in the thought of Panikkar and Devanandan. Especially criticisms raised from within their respective Catholic and Protestant theological circles where their concern for interfaith dialogue is appreciated and broadly shared. We may do this under two main heads — the relation of the historical-particular to the universal, and the relation of soteriology to anthropology.

The historical and the universal

The emphasis on the universal Christ is made in order to find a common ground for particular historical religions to meet and enter into dialogue with one another. The universality may be interpreted in mystical metaphysical-ontological or mythical-cosmic terms. The question most often asked is as to whether Panikkar's universal Christ does not dissolve the essential unique historicity of the revelation of God in Jesus of Nazareth.

The Indian theologian Anto Karokaran, while commending Panikkar for opening up the question of inter-religious relations in a radical way, and agreeing with much in Panikkar's theology, joins issue with him for weakening if not eliminating the historical dimension of religion.

> It is relevant to note that Panikkar, in order to establish his thesis, has taken great pains to show the limitations of the historical dimension of religion. Whenever he speaks about the historical dimension of religion, he dwells on

> its negative aspect although he does not absolutely deny the need for such a dimension. But by constantly harping on the limitations, he creates the impression that the historical dimension as applied to religion is more a liability than an asset.[1]

Karokaran illustrates this through an examination of Panikkar's conceptions of Christ and the church. He notes that while Panikkar "has volumes to say on the Unknown Christ he has comparatively little to say about the Known Christ. While he cleverly manages to decipher the hidden face of God in other religions, his reading of the revealed face of God in Christianity is not so fascinating. While he shows at length how Christ has been revealing himself in his immanent or ontic capacity and how he would reveal himself fully at the final *parousia*, he is very sparing in explaining the revelation which Christ has made of himself in history." And this has robbed God's revelation in Christ of its unique character as "the most decisive factor for every man in determining his relation to the ultimate reality".

According to Karokaran, this is true also of his concept of Christianity. For Panikkar "the identity of a religion" does not include "a historical social set-up" to express and communicate its vision of ultimate reality: the church, therefore, lacks any real actualization in history.

Karokaran does not deny the reality of the "ontic Christ". But in his opinion, "we have no reason to conclude that his (Christ's) meeting with man in history is something outside his meeting with man on the ontic level; on the other hand we have to understand that the ontic relation is included also in the historical act of revelation."[2]

Hans Küng criticizes Panikkar for making the "Cosmic Christ" his starting point for interfaith dialogue, because it de-emphasizes the historical dimension of the Christ-event. He is especially critical of Panikkar's attempt in the *Unknown Christ of Hinduism* (1964) at comparing classical Indian texts relating Brahman (the Absolute, Transcendent, the Unknown) to Eswara (Lord, Creator, God) to the relation between God the Father and God the Son in the Christian doctrine of the Trinity.

Küng wonders whether Panikkar is "doing justice to Indian ideas" when he compares "one speculation with another in the manner that is still too Western". He adds:

> On the Christian side, this sort of comparison presupposes a fully developed doctrine of the Trinity, which we do not hear about until the Neo-Nicene fathers around the end of the fourth century, and which has little to do with the Jesus of the Synoptic Gospels, who never hinted of such a "mystery".

> Panikkar, too, might well have had doubts here. Are we to burden Indians with all this highly developed Hellenistic dogma? Is this what an Indian Christian theology will be like? If so, it will be a far cry from the Jesus of the Gospels, not to mention historical criticisms of the Bible and Christian tradition.[3]

It would be wrong for religious truth to minimize "the structural differences" between Hinduism which sees God, humanity and world primarily in "a natural-cyclical context" and Christianity which views them in "a historical process".

> Jesus is not a mythical figure, not a divine being that takes on an earthly body for a given time, not a symbol of supernatural truth without a trace of historical singularity. The message of the New Testament fastens Christian faith (despite some mythical language) to a real person, a quite specific historical figure, Jesus of Nazareth, whose message and life are the divine criteria for faith and activity, living and dying of Christians because he is God's unique revelation.[4]

This also has consequences of "the greatest significance for the problems facing the individual and society". Therefore, "as opposed to speculative theological mediation", Küng would join with all the Indian theologians and exegetes whose point of departure has been "the concrete Jesus of the Sermon of the Mount and the Way of the Cross".[5] This would make it possible to "relate Jesus Christ both to Brahma and the world" and to bring "the dimension of the personal and the historical" into Hindu spirituality.[6]

Of course the issue at debate here is how the Bible relates mythology and history in its essential tradition, and more particularly how the New Testament sees the relation between myth and history in the Christ-event. The general consensus among biblical scholars at present seems to be that while myths and history are interwoven in the Bible, the pressure of the faith of Israel and the church is in the direction of demythologization and the historicization of myths, transforming them into symbols and memorials of historical events embodying divine promise and fulfilment for the future. For example Brevand Childs speaks about "broken myth" in which the biblical writers either historicize mythical material or use it merely as an extended figure of speech. Gerhard von Rad understands Israel as breaking through to a concept of linear history. Wolfhart Pannenberg sees the use of myth by Israel and early Christianity to be primarily typological in its function and made to serve the history of the saving acts of God. Frank Cross explains the uniqueness of Israel's religion as lying in the tension between myth and history where myth serves to give "cosmic dimension and transcendent meaning to the historical".[7]

However, this consensus has been challenged from the side of the History of Religion. Following Mircea Eliade's *Cosmos and History*[8] and *The Quest: the History and Meaning in Religion*,[9] historians of religion tend to interpret all religions including biblical religion as attempts to overcome the terrors of history by converting "historical time" into "mythical time". This approach points out that the perception of the centrality of historicity may in part be the result of a certain misreading of the biblical material. It has been argued that in "the biblical material that can be connected with specific rituals (the New Year Festival, Covenant Renewal Festival, Passover, Advent of the Divine Warrior, Holy War, Temple liturgies, and Lord's Supper)" the concept of time is "overwhelmingly mythical in nature", mythical time being understood here in terms of Eliade's idea of being involved in "the cyclic regeneration of time" through rituals celebrating "the myth of the eternal return" to origins. Even the re-dramatization, in cult, of the redemptive acts of Yahweh, i.e. the Exodus, Sinai and the Conquest, while valuing history, may be seen also as bringing them into a kind of "cosmogonic or historical" primordiality of sacredness as contrasted with the "pre-cosmic" kind.[10]

The relation between the mythical and the historical in the biblical faith needs to be pursued further. But Eliade himself has said that "the central role of Jesus, as Christ" in "the entire corpus of myths, rituals, and beliefs" of the Christian religion, is "transparent".[11]

In the context of this discussion, the criticism by Nirmal Minz, a Protestant Indian theologian, of Devanandan's emphasis on the historical particularity of Jesus, and on historical and personal categories of humanness in his theology of dialogue, is worth noting. While admitting that Devanandan took a major step forward in the development of a theology which would enable the church to relate the gospel to the changed cultural situation of pluralism in India, Minz is critical of it at various points.

First, the missionary motivation which is dominant in Devanandan's theology makes it too "defensive", and makes the justification of Christian faith its "final aim". This precludes the "elemental openness and willingness necessary for understanding the other as an equal partner in the dialogue". Secondly, Devanandan's preoccupation with the "personal and historical categories" makes his theology inadequate to meet "the metaphysically oriented" Hindu partner in real dialogue "on the conceptual level". Minz points out that this may be one reason why many interfaith meetings in India so far have been "parallel monologues". He says: "Neither a pure metaphysical approach of the Hindu philosopher-theologian nor a pure historical and personalistic emphasis of the Indian Christian theologian is of much help in the present Hindu-Christian dialogue in India... Both sides need to learn to see and to give meaning to reality on three levels. There is the factual, the symbolic and the spiritual meaning of any given fact or event in human experience. Participants in dialogue need to meet their partners on all these levels on conversations and interpenetrations." Thirdly, and this Minz repeats in various ways, Devanandan's "neo-orthodox stance" makes his theology of religious pluralism weak at many points. The neo-orthodox "suspicion of human reason and culture" lies behind the unwillingness to take the metaphysical-ontological realm of religious discourse seriously. It also prevents Devanandan from spelling out God's witness and the presence of Christ *incognito* in other religious traditions. Fourthly, Devanandan dogmatically takes for granted that "Jesus Christ is the starting point and criterion of judgment" in all theological and anthropological matters. This approach, says Minz, "provides no meaningful way to interpret the two sets of realities which are brought into focus in a Hindu-Christian dialogue situation".[12]

A good many Christian thinkers have taken to the "theocentric model" to avoid the problems inherent in the Jesus-oriented Christo-centricism to which Nirmal Minz here refers. But if the central motive for dialogue is provided by the present historical situation with its demand to build a more genuine human community which recognizes plurality, we cannot dispose of the spiritual significance of human history as a marginal theme in interfaith dialogue. It is central. If it is, does not the unique humanity of Jesus crucified and risen as the power of being human and the source of renewal for historical existence remain the most important contribution in and to the dialogue of religions and secular ideologies?

Salvation and humanization

The theology of Devanandan was criticized at New Delhi 1961 and after from the perspective of European Neo-orthodoxy. Primarily because he emphasized the awakening of non-Christian religions to the "new anthropology" of personal values, social justice in community and purposive history under the impact of Christianity and Western culture as reflecting the presence of Christ and the renewing work of the Holy Spirit, even when they were separated from the church's proclamation of the gospel of forgiveness in Jesus Christ. If I remember correctly, Edmund Schlink at New Delhi made the point that the presence of Christ and the Spirit *accompanied* the church's historical act of the preaching of repentance and forgiveness and did not precede it. This and similar contributions to the discussion on the report on "witness" led to changing the wording of an earlier draft on other faiths. The earlier draft spoke of the church being sent to proclaim Christ as Lord and Saviour to all nations and in all spheres of life "knowing that the Spirit of God is already at work amongst men, preparing for the coming of the gospel", and added: "In the churches we have but little understanding of the wisdom, love and power God has given to men of other faiths and of no faith or of the change wrought in other faiths by their long encounter with Christianity. We must take up the conversation about Christ with them, knowing that Christ meets us in them."[13] This was changed to read as follows:

> The Church is sent knowing that God has not left himself without witness even among men who do not know Christ and knowing also that the reconciliation wrought through Christ embraces all creation and the whole of mankind. We are aware that this great truth has implications when we go out to meet men of other faiths. But there are differences of opinion amongst us when we attempt to define the relation and response of such men to the activity of God amongst them... In the churches we have but little understanding of the wisdom, love and power which God has given to men of other faiths by their long encounter with Christianity. We must take up the conversation about Christ with them, knowing that Christ addresses them through us and us through them.[14]

The warning one finds in the same report against identifying Christ with any historical movement of change came partly out of this fear of separating movements of human renewal from the proclamation of divine forgiveness in Jesus Christ and eventually making humanization the sole content of salvation. It says that while "as Christians we believe that God is at work in all the great changes which are taking place in our age",

> we must resist the temptation to see the hand of God in the particular movements of history of which we personally approve or to claim his blessing for every cause which seems righteous at the moment. We may nevertheless proclaim in such situations the Lordship of Christ over the whole process which is changing the aspect of our world.[15]

But without some discernment of what is of God in the changing situation and what is not, how do Christians participate in historical action?

H.H. Wolf's article "Christ at Work in History — in the Light of the Barmen Declaration of the Confessing Church of Germany"[16], criticizing the idea of discerning the work of Christ among mankind "apart from and outside the actual preaching of the gospel", illustrated and expressed more clearly the neo-orthodox nervousness to which Schlink and others gave expression in New Delhi.

This nervousness also led to the strengthening of two dangerous conservative evangelical tendencies — one to define salvation in purely individualistic terms denying its social and cosmic reach; and the other to isolate soteriology from anthropology and thereby to compartmentalize salvation history and secular history. The Lausanne Covenant adopted by the Lausanne Conference of Evangelicals in 1974 recognizes Christians' responsibility to serve society and promote justice and peace, but sees it only as a "consequence" of salvation and not as "constitutive" of it.[17] John Stott's *Christian Mission in the Modern World*[18] underlines this point. In the Lausanne follow-up study on gospel and culture, there is a condemnation of the "most insidious" form of syncretism which "mixes a privatized gospel of personal forgiveness with a worldly (even demonic) attitude to wealth and power".[19] But there is no recognition that it might be the result of the stance of a purely privatized personal understanding of salvation.

Through the years Lesslie Newbigin has sought to clarify to fellow evangelicals the relation between the historical particularity of the election of Christ and the church and the universally human and cosmic reach of the salvation in Christ.[20] He has also given recognition, too cautiously perhaps, to Devanandan's approach of discerning Christ in the ferment of human renewal in India and of speaking of soteriology within the context of and in the medium of the new anthropology. Discussing a model of inter-religious dialogue based on the practical need for political and social life, Newbigin mentions the classic example of the Mughal emperor Akbar and adds:

> India since 1947 has again witnessed the strong pressure of the mood for national unity upon the thinking of responsible people in the various religious communities. This pressure can be understood in a superficial way which simply subordinates concern for truth in religion to a concern for political unity. But it can also be understood in a more fundamental way. Outstanding Christian thinkers such as Paul Devanandan... saw both the renaissance of Hinduism and the growth of a concern for nation-building were part of the consequences of the impact of Christ upon Indian society. They therefore called their fellow Christians to the work of interfaith dialogue in the context

> of the quest for national unity with the conviction that this was part of the continuing work of Christ in Indian society. The basis of their call to dialogue was in their Christian faith.[21]

Pannenberg has spoken more clearly about anthropology being the medium of fundamental theological discourse and the explication of salvation in Christ in this age. Theological anthropology, he says, "nowadays has the status of a form of fundamental theology".[22]

The relation between salvation and humanization also needs deeper ecumenical exploration. Is not the ultimate salvation an "eschatological humanization" where sin, principalities and powers, and death will be removed and humanity will find divine fulfilment in the kingdom (Cor. 15:20-28)? And, therefore, are not Jesus' resurrection and its humanizing power this side of death, the "first fruits" (1 Cor. 15:20; James. 1:18) of the ultimate salvation?

The historical and anthropological questions in our time have been raised most radically by modern secular humanistic ideologies. In fact all traditional religions including Christianity have been challenged by them to renew themselves. It was this perception that led the World Council of Churches to emphasize that the programme of the dialogue sub-unit should include both religious faiths and secular ideologies.

It seems that dialogue with secular ideologies has now been separated from inter-religious dialogue. The Vatican had made the separation from the very beginning.

But such separation has resulted in inter-religious dialogue becoming oriented to traditional religions rather than to religions in their renascent phase of awareness of the historical situation. Consequently it has become easier to avoid the crucial questions of the spiritual significance of the corporate secular structures in the scheme of salvation, questions which modern ideologies have sharply raised. The trend could also halt the renewal of secular ideologies in the light of transcendence. One of the crucial questions which needs ecumenical exploration in interfaith dialogue in our time is the nature of the partnership we must have with ideologies of secular humanism.

Church and the wider koinonia-in-Christ

Both Panikkar and Devanandan seek to go beyond the idea of Christianity as one religion over against other religions and quasi-religions and to see it as the sign of the kingdom and the fermenting leaven in the universe of faiths bringing to them the transforming knowledge of the universal presence of the Christ of God, the mediator of human and cosmic salvation. In this search, they outline the features not only of a Christ who is more than the Jesus of Nazareth but also a people of Christ in world history which is more than the historical community of those openly acknowledging Jesus as God and Saviour. Panikkar's "Unknown Christ" of traditional faiths and Devanandan's "acknowledged Christ" of the renascent faiths may have to be redefined; but they point to a reality which call for a redefinition of the church of Jesus Christ in relation to a wider people of the Christ.

The nature of the church has been the central subject of consideration in Christian ecumenism through the years. The church has always been defined in relation to God's purpose for the whole of humanity — either in terms of God's mission of salvation to an alienated humanity or, more recently, as "the sign and sacrament" of an already ontologically existing unity or a historical "coming unity" of humanity (Vatican II and Uppsala 1968). These formulations remain valid. But the discernment of faith-responses to Christ outside the church and the need for Christians to be in dialogical partnership with others in the witness to the kingdom to come call for a redefinition of the different levels and forms of koinonia-in-Christ in history and the relation between them in Christian living and the Christian mission of humanization and salvation. This is an important ecumenical task for our generation.

We shall continue to speak of the community of those openly acknowledging the crucified and risen Jesus as the Christ and gathered round the Lord's Table and the exposition of the word of God and scattered for witness and service, as the *church*, the "structured nucleus" of the people of Christ. But we have also to acknowledge a larger "unstructured stream" of koinonia-in-Christ or communion in the Messiah in human history, which is spiritually continuous and discontinuous with it. Mahatma Gandhi once said of Jesus:

> The lives for all of us have, in some greater or lesser degree, been changed by his presence, his actions and the word spoken by his divine voice... And because the life of Jesus has had the significance and the transcendence to which I have alluded, I believe that he belongs not solely to Christianity but to the entire world, to all races and people; it matters little under what flag, name or doctrine they may work, profess a faith or worship a God inherited from their ancestors.[23]

Further, the "lamb slain" who is "on the throne" at the End is present "from the foundation of the world" (Rev. 13:8). Despite demons of self-righteousness and self-aggression the cross or the self-emptying redemptive love of God revealed in Jesus has been the central dynamic of all history. "The light shines in darkness and the darkness has not overcome it" (John 1:5). John V. Taylor goes even further when he sees the principle of the cross, of life through self-sacrifice, present and at work side by side with the principle of self-aggression, in the whole creation process, including that of nature and society. He says: "The free obedience of Jesus, his dying for us all and his rising again, are both history and universal reality."[24] It is the crucified and risen Jesus who is our evidence that "we are citizens of a forgiven universe", and that being-in-Christ is the "primary and essential condition of man's existence". This is clearly declared in the New Testament hymns of creation in John 1, Colossians 1, and Hebrews 1, and in the creeds where "all things" are seen as having been created through Christ and by him, and as subsisting in him and oriented towards him. Such a universal presence of Christ also posits the possibility and the reality of people being saved "not by relating only to that historical life, death and resurrection in which the pattern was made plain, once for all, but by relating also to the pattern wherever it emerges" in the tissue of historical existence — not merely religious existence, but just human existence, religious or secular, and not only in contemporary history, but in the whole history of humanity. This is what gives validity to all our talk of the Unknown Christ, Anonymous Christianity and the latent church. But the historical cross remains the clue, the criterion for discerning the stirrings and positive responses of faith to the universal cross. And therefore, as Schillebeeckx says, they are "the initial stage — something which of its nature requires to grow to completion" in the acknowledgment of the dialectic between the historical and the universal in Jesus Christ.[25]

This means that several kinds of implicit faith-response to Christ, without explicit acknowledgment of Jesus as the Christ, could well be included in the wider koinonia-in-Christ. As in these examples. The pattern of secular self-giving love and forgiveness, with an openness to the realm of transcendent forgiveness. A faith in the holy with the expectation of a divine mediation of love or the atonement of a suffering Messiah. A recognition of the person of Jesus as the ultimate pattern of the Messiah to come. The experience of mystic union where there is a recognition of mutual indwelling between human persons and the divine person. The self-commitment to the cause of creating a community of persons on earth envisaged as faith overcoming death. And more.

C.F. Andrews, writing to Tambaram 1938, said that the mission of the church involved "not merely to quicken those who are dead in trespasses but also to welcome with joy his radiant presence in those who have seen from afar his glory".[26] The church's recognition of and dialogue with this wider koinonia-in-Christ are spiritually necessary for both. On the one hand, it will save the church from the kind of spiritual egoism which arrogates to itself the right to decide who belongs to the messianic people, and it can bring to the church an awareness of hitherto unexplored insights and facets of life in the Holy Spirit. On the other, through the encounter with the Person of Jesus Christ, commitments to the universal Christ-principle and the way of the cross could escape the danger of being perverted into legalism and used as instruments of self-justification.

An ecumenical problem

It is clear from our survey that Panikkar and Devanandan cannot be understood apart from the Catholic and Protestant church traditions in which they take their respective stand even while going beyond them. This leads us to observe that the difference between their Christologies and theologies of religions reflects the traditional Catholic-Protestant theological conflict which has been dominant in the history of Western Christianity. It refers to the relation between Nature and Grace. Only it takes on different forms, like the relation between religion and revelation, or between nature and history, or between the realms of the sacred and the secular. Therefore, the reconciliation of the Christologies of Panikkar and Devanandan is more than just the reconciliation of two thinkers; it involves the reconciliation of two theological traditions. In fact it is a problem of interchurch ecumenism at its deepest.

Paul Verghese (now Metroplitan Paulos Mar Gregorios), in some of his observations on the debate on secularization, has brought this fact to our attention.[27] According to him, Western culture in all its different traditions reflects "a dichotomous view of reality as divided into nature and supernature". This started with medieval Catholic theology and is clearly reflected in the Catholic-Protestant debates during and after the Reformation. It dominates Western theology so much that Karl Barth and Karl Rahner both theologize within this framework. Both characterize the realm of nature as "that which we can experience and understand without revelation", as "a self-contained realm which operates by its own principles", and distinguish it from the "realm of revelation, grace or supernature where it operates through laws of a different order"; and the debate centres round the relation between the two which have been separated into "parallel layers" as a result of the obscuring of the gospel of the incarnation in Western culture.

In modern cultural history this separation produced "two deviations in thought" which became firmly established — namely the hiatus between humanity and the universe and between divine grace and human nature. Hegel and Marx may be said to have "put together what medieval theology and Kant had set apart. But in that process the transcendent has disappeared and man became caged in a self-created universe."[28] And the history of Western theology shows "how difficult it is for people living in a certain culture to move out of its basic assumptions".

Mar Gregorios is not discussing Panikkar and Devanandan. But given the above approach, he will see the conflict between the Catholic and Protestant traditions they represent as reflecting the contradiction of a Western Christianity built on the division of reality into nature and supernature. The incarnation, in the tradition of the church fathers preserved by Eastern Christianity, rejects this notion.

> The Incarnation bears witness to the salvation of the universe in its entirety. Man is not saved *from* his materiality but rather *in* it. His salvation is not a total disruption of all historical processes by superhistorical intervention, but a radical transformation of the process of history by the transcendent God entering history in an immanent way through the Body of Christ.
>
> The Incarnation is a basic affirmation of materiality and of things human. There is no longer an unbridgeable gap between the transcendent God and the created order, because the gap has already been bridged by God who has entered the created order bodily. In this view the Church is also a "consecrating" presence, not merely an over-against presence in the world.[29]

Therefore, "the meaning of the Incarnation in which God has *become* man, thus becoming one with the creation and yet not ceasing to be God, thus remaining transcendent from the creation and not totally merged in the creation" must determine church-world relations. The "notions of *community* (the koinonia in the Trinity), *pluralism* (the Holy Spirit — giver of diverse gifts) and *humanity* (the Son of God who became man) are rooted in the fundamentals of the Christian faith".[30] Here, of course, Eastern Orthodoxy is presented as uniting the ontic and the historical in the Incarnate Christ and his body the church.

Metropolitan George Khodr of Lebanon is another Eastern Orthodox theologian who has sought to criticize the Western theology of "salvation history" and to spell out the Eastern theology of church in relation to religions. In his speech at the Addis Ababa Central Committee of the World Council of Churches he said:

> The church is the medium of the mystery of the nations' salvation. She is the sign of God's love for all men. She is not set over against the world of

> which, from one point of view, she is a part. Rather she is the very heart of mankind, the image of mankind to come, thanks to the light she has received. She is the life of men even if these are unaware, the "cosmos of the cosmos" as Origen puts it. If the Son, as Origen also says, is the "cosmos of the Church" then the Church's function must be so to read, in the light of the mystery she signifies, all the other signs that God has set in the passing years, even in the religions, that she can make known to the world of the religions the God who is hidden in it and so bring on the final and actual unfolding of that mystery.[31]

Is there the possibility of a reconciliation of the nature-supernature, religion-revelation, history-ontology debate between Catholicism and Protestantism through Eastern Orthodoxy? Perhaps; but only after Eastern Orthodox theology itself reckons with the separation of nature, humanity, and God, and assimilates the positive values of this separation while rejecting its perversions — and thereby renews itself.

It is clear however that Christian ecumenism must take the theology of religious pluralism as an important theme of interchurch dialogues. Now that the churches are finding a large measure of convergence on "Baptism, Eucharist and Ministry" it is time to develop interchurch understanding at other levels, like the theology of social ethics and the theology of religions where theological differences remain crucial. In fact even the convergence in "Baptism, Eucharist and Ministry" has yet to be tested in the context of the theology of church-world relations in a pluralistic global setting.

The churches of Africa and Asia are only beginning to enter into dialogue with their own indigenous religious and cultural contexts which are different from the Latin-Greek-Semitic ones. They are also grappling with the social and ethical problems of technological culture. The Christologies and forms of church life which will emerge in this process cannot be foreseen. Nor should they be decided by the authority of the consensus arrived at among the traditional Catholic-Orthodox-Protestant theologies.

Further, many theologians in Asia are convinced that an ecumenical theology of religion cannot just be the product of interconfessional dialogue on dogmatic orthodoxy. It can emerge only as a result of dialogue among Christians and churches involved in orthopraxis, that is common involvement with adherents of all religions and secular ideologies in the Asian people's struggle to realize full humanity. This is often articulated in the meetings of theologians and among the Christian social action groups in the third world.

According to J. Russell Chandran, who was for a number of years the president of the Ecumenical Association of Third World Theologians, "true theology is not just a process of formulation of doctrines, but a process of doing, a process of participation in the real presence of Christ with two poles, one the sacramental participation and the other a contemporary re-enactment of the exodus-covenant experience for people suffering under different forms of oppression".[32] Aloysius Pieris S.J. of Sri Lanka makes the same point in a slightly different way. He says that "theo-praxis is already the formulation of theology". Theo-praxis means that the church follows the path of "the transcendence of the crucified God" in Jesus to God's kingdom through an identification with the people's struggle for spiritual and social emancipation. This involves the church in a double-baptism, one "in the Jordan of Asian religiosity" and the other "on the cross of Asian poverty", for the sake of "dynamic participation" in the people's struggle for full humanity.[33] The "theology of the people" developed by the Christian Conference of Asia (CCA) also moves along the same line.

Now to sum up. If the New Humanity in Christ is to transcend Christianity, other religions, and atheistic ideologies, it must transform them all from within, and it can then take new and diverse forms in them. Thus unity in Christ has to be seen as resulting from inner reform and should accommodate diversity. It seems also to envisage three levels of koinonia in Christ: first, the koinonia of the eucharistic community of the church, itself a unity of diverse peoples acknowledging the *Person* of Jesus as the Messiah; second, a larger koinonia of dialogue among people of different faiths inwardly being renewed by their acknowledgment of the ultimacy of the *pattern* of suffering servanthood as exemplified by the crucified Jesus; third, a still larger koinonia of those involved in the power-political struggle for new societies and a world community based on secular or religious anthropologies *informed by* the agape of the cross. The spiritual tension between them seems to be essential for the health of all of them and for the development of a Christology, Christian mission and forms of church life more adequate for and relevant to our pluralistic age.

The theology of religious pluralism is indeed an ecumenical issue of great importance — and of great consequences — in our time.

NOTES

[1] *Evangelism and Diakonia*, Bangalore, Dharmaran, 1978, pp.308-309.
[2] *Ibid.*, p.20.
[3] *Christianity and the World Religions*, Garden City, NY, Doubleday, 1986, p.275.
[4] *Ibid.*, pp.279-280.
[5] *Ibid.*, p.280.
[6] *Ibid.*, p.279.

[7] Childs, *Myth and Reality in the Old Testament*, London, SCM, 1960, pp.30-71. Von Rad, *Old Testament Theology II*, New York, Harper & Row, 1965, pp.99-113. Pannenberg, *The Idea of God and Human Freedom*, Philadelphia, Westminster, 1973, pp.1-80. Cross, *Canaanite Myth and Hebrew Epic*, Cambridge, MA, Harvard University, 1973, pp.79-90.

[8] New York, Harper, 1959.

[9] Chicago, University of Chicago, 1969.

[10] References here are to an unpublished paper: *Mythosgeschichte: Common Ground on Which to Begin Dialogue in a Pluralistic World*, Chip Dobbs-Allsopp, Princeton.

[11] *The Quest, op. cit.*, p.10.

[12] *Mahatma Gandhi and Hindu-Christian Dialogue*, Bangalore, CISRS, pp.132-135.

[13] Assembly document No. 74, p.16.

[14] *New Delhi Report*, New York, Associated Press, 1962, pp.81-82.

[15] *Ibid.*, p.85.

[16] *The Ecumenical Review*, January 1966.

[17] The Lausanne Covenant: an Exposition and Commentary by John Stott, Minneapolis, World-wide, 1975.

[18] London, Falcon, 1975.

[19] *The Willow Bank Report: Report of a Consultation on Gospel and Culture*, Wheaton, Lausanne Committee, 1978.

[20] *The Open Secret*, Grand Rapids, Eerdmans, 1978, pp.73-101.

[21] Ed. Richard W. Rousseau, SJ, *Inter-religious Dialogue: Facing the Next Frontier*, Vol. I, Scranton, Ridge Row, 1981, p.15.

[22] *The Idea of God and Human Freedom*, Philadelphia, Westminster, 1973, p.90.

[23] *Modern Review*, Calcutta, 1941.

[24] *The Go-Between God*, London, SCM, 1973, p.180.

[25] *Christ the Sacrament of the Encounter With God*, New York, Sheed & Ward, 1963, pp.178-179.

[26] Quoted by Chaturvedi and Sykes, *Charles Freer Andrews*, foreword by M.K. Gandhi, London, Allen & Unwin, 1949, p.311.

[27] "Dialogue with Secularism", ed. H. Jai Singh, *Inter-religious Dialogue*, Bangalore, CISRS, 1967, pp.225-229.

[28] *Ibid.*, p.229.

[29] *Ibid.*, p.231.

[30] *Ibid.*, p.237.

[31] Ed. S.J. Samartha, *Living Faiths and the Ecumenical Movement*, Geneva, WCC, 1971, p.137.

[32] Torres and Fabella, eds, *The Emerging Gospel: Theology from the Underside of History*, Maryknoll, Orbis, 1976, p.171.

[33] Ed. Douglas Elwood, *Asian Christian Theology*, Philadelphia, Westminster Press, 1980, pp.239-251.

Index of Names